Easy Suppers

HPBooks

Easy
Suppers

Pat Jester

ANOTHER BEST-SELLING VOLUME FROM H.P. BOOKS

Editorial Director: Helen Fisher; Editor: Carlene Tejada; Art Director: Don Burton; Book Assembly: Ken Heiden; Typography: Cindy Coatsworth, Joanne Nociti, Patty Thompson; Research Assistant: Karla Tillotson; Food Stylists: Pat Jester, Karla Tillotson; Photography: George deGennaro Studios—George deGennaro, David Wong, Dennis Skinner, Tom Miyasaki.

Published by H.P. Books, P.O. Box 5367, Tucson, AZ 85703 602/888-2150
ISBN 0-89586-064-3
Library of Congress Catalog Card Number 80-82384
© 1980 Fisher Publishing, Inc.
Printed in U.S.A.

Cover Photo: Shortcut Spaghetti Supper, page 14

Easy Suppers is for you!

You're overwhelmed with the fast pace of everday living. There never seems to be enough time! If every member of your household has joined the ranks of wage earners or devotes blocks of time to school, hobbies or volunteer work, who's minding the kitchen? You probably depend on the coffee wagon, fast-food restaurants and frozen dinners and you worry about nutrition. Or maybe you spend hours trying to organize incompatible foods into an acceptable supper. When you end up throwing out most of it, you feel you've wasted your evening.

You can make better use of your time. What you need are fast easy recipes, menu planning ideas and shopping suggestions.

That's what *Easy Suppers* is all about. With the recipes, menus and tips in this book, you can cook creatively even when you're short of time or too tired to prepare an appetizing meal from scratch. Some recipes require a little advance preparation or shopping. But—let's admit it—a delicious quick-as-a-minute meal served with a gourmet touch is worth a few extra minutes.

As you look through this book, you may find your perspective changing. First of all, you don't need to serve a five-course meal to keep your family well-nourished or to entertain your guests. Keep it light and simple. Meal preparation will be easier and faster if you don't make every item on your menu from a recipe. Make ahead whenever time permits. If you have even one food item on your menu tucked away in the refrigerator or freezer, you're well on your way to an easy supper you'll be proud to serve.

When planning your menu, consider the main dish first. Use the rest of the meal to highlight the main dish. Contrast shapes, textures and temperatures of foods as well as their colors and flavors.

Use one of these ideas to cut down on work and add a gourmet touch to your next supper:
● Store several varieties of canned fruit in the refrigerator. Serve the cold fruit on lettuce leaves as a salad or in small bowls for dessert.
● Make a frozen salad mold and keep it tightly wrapped in the freezer. It will be a colorful and refreshing surprise at the end of a hectic day.
● Freeze several kinds of breads and rolls, including French bread. When you need a special

bread to complete a meal, you can go right to your freezer.
● Marinated artichokes, spiced peaches, spiced crabapples, pickles, olives or pickled beets are indispensable for a quick relish tray. Choose two or three of your favorites and add fresh celery or carrot sticks or zucchini wedges.
● Keep three or four bottled salad dressings chilled. Choose one to drizzle over lettuce wedges or fresh or canned tomato slices, then sprinkle with salad seasoning. You can also marinate hot cooked vegetables in salad dressing.
● Few foods offer such wonderful versatility as cheese. Keep several kinds on hand to shred over salads or vegetables, to serve with crackers and soup as a first course, or to arrange with fresh fruit on a dessert tray with coffee or wine.
● Always have vanilla ice cream in your freezer. Layer it with frozen fruit in parfait glasses, pour liqueur over it, whirl it in the blender for a drink base or scoop it on brownies or cake. Try rolling scoops of ice cream in chopped nuts and drizzle with caramel topping.
● Assorted packaged rice mixes, potato mixes and frozen vegetables will give you a wide range of choices. Mix and match potato or rice dishes with vegetables and meat, chicken or fish.
● Canned sliced mushrooms, chopped pimiento, and croutons add distinctive touches to vegetables, salads and packaged or frozen dinner mixes.
● Maintain a well-stocked shelf of seasonings. Instant minced onion, dried parsley, celery and pepper flakes, seasoned salts, herbs and spices bring new and exciting flavors to standard dishes. Use the recipes in this book as a guide, then experiment on your own.
● Canned chicken and beef broth are marvelous as flavor boosters. Use them instead of water to make soup, rice and sauces.

With these basic supplies and quick and easy techniques, you are ready to begin. Before you start, turn the page. Menu suggestions on the following pages show how to combine recipes, convenience foods and canned and frozen foods to make an enjoyable meal with a minimum of preparation. *Easy Suppers* can improve your lifestyle. So don't put it off another evening—it's time you enjoyed an *easy* supper!

Make-Ahead Buffet is pictured on the following pages. From top right: Pistachio Torte, page 9; Buffet Ham Slices, page 8; Pickled Peaches, page 94; Herbed Macaroni Salad, page 9.

Pat Jester

Pat Jester knows what she's talking about. As a career woman who runs a home and loves good food, Pat discovered that the worst time of day can be the hour or so you're trying to prepare an appetizing, nourishing supper after a long day at work. She began to take special notice of packaged and convenience foods available in supermarkets and specialty food shops. The next step was to develop recipes that used these foods to their best advantage. Along the way she collected ideas and information for cooking, combining, assembling and serving these easily prepared foods. In *Easy Suppers*, Pat shares this information with you.

Since her days at Iowa State University, Pat has been creating new recipes. From dietary work in hospitals, she went on to recipe development and food styling for large food corporations. She also develops instruction booklets and sales literature for various kitchen appliances. Pat has long been associated with Better Homes and Gardens publications as a columnist and editor.

At her own company, Creative Foods, Ltd., in Des Moines, Iowa, Pat and her staff develop and test new recipes and do food styling for educational and advertising projects. Several well-known companies use Pat's expertise in their promotional booklets.

Holiday Late Supper

This flexible menu accommodates even the wee-hours-of-the-morning stragglers. Have the egg mixture for the omelets mixed and stored in your refrigerator. As each person comes home, ladle a generous portion of egg mixture into melted butter in a skillet. Raid the refrigerator for fillings or make any of the fillings on pages 72 to 76.

Salad can be made ahead and kept fresh in the refrigerator. Put the dressing in a screw-top jar and shake it well before pouring it over each serving of salad.

Menu
Make-Your-Own Omelets, pages 72 to 76
Naturally Good Salad, page 90
Posh Pan Rolls, page 119
Butter   Jam
Frozen Pumpkin Pie
Coffee

Frozen Pumpkin Pie

Holiday pie was never this easy!

1/2 cup graham cracker crumbs
1 cup canned pumpkin
1/2 cup packed brown sugar
1 teaspoon pumpkin pie spice

1 cup frozen whipped dessert topping, thawed
1 pint butter brickle ice cream, softened
1/3 cup chopped pecans
Caramel ice cream topping

Sprinkle graham cracker crumbs over the bottom of a 9-inch pie plate. In a medium bowl, mix pumpkin, brown sugar, and pumpkin pie spice. Fold in whipped topping. Spoon softened ice cream on top of crumbs in pie plate. Top with pumpkin mixture. Sprinkle with pecans. Freeze. Let stand 10 minutes at room temperature before serving. Cut in wedges. Drizzle with caramel sauce. Makes 6 servings.

Make Ahead Buffet

What a delightful make-ahead buffet this is! You can cook the ham, make the macaroni salad, pickle the peaches and assemble the torte up to two days before the party. Your only last-minute details are heating brown-and-serve rolls and making coffee.

Your guests will enjoy helping themselves at your special spritzer bar. Set out lemon and lime slices with chilled soda water, chilled Chablis, chilled dry vermouth and creme de cassis. Try the European favorite *Kir*—a dash of cassis in the bottom of the glass topped with Chablis. For a variation on a martini, substitute vermouth for Chablis. Or mix Chablis and fruit slices with a generous splash of soda water to create a true spritzer. For those watching their weight, there's always soda water—imported to give your party continental airs—with a refreshing wedge of lime on the side.

Menu

Make-Your-Own Spritzers
Buffet Ham Slices
Herbed Macaroni Salad
Pickled Peaches, page 94
Hot Crusty Rolls   Butter
Pistachio Torte
Coffee

Buffet Ham Slices   Photo on pages 4 and 5.

Cooking the ham in its own container adds to the convenience.

1 (5-lb.) canned ham in metal can
1/2 (6-oz.) can frozen pineapple-orange juice
  concentrate, thawed (1/3 cup)

1/3 cup maple-flavored syrup
1/3 cup dry white wine

Preheat oven to 325°F (165°C). Open canned ham and remove lid. Unwrap ham if it is in a paper wrapping. Pour off liquid from ham. Place ham back in can and cover with foil. Place can in a foil-lined shallow baking pan and place in oven. Bake 30 minutes. Pour off liquid and return can to foil-lined pan. In a small bowl, mix juice concentrate, syrup and wine. Pour over ham. Cover loosely with foil. Continue cooking 2 to 2-1/2 hours. Slice ham and serve warm. Or chill, then slice and serve cold. Makes 12 servings.

Pistachio Torte   *Photo on pages 4 and 5.*

At holiday time, garnish this lavish green torte with bright red cranberries or strawberries.

1 (3-3/4-oz.) pkg. instant pistachio pudding mix	1 envelope whipped topping mix
1 cup cold milk	1 cup cold milk
1 (10-3/4-oz.) frozen pound cake, thawed	1/2 teaspoon vanilla extract
	Chopped pistachio nuts

Measure 1/3 cup dry pudding mix into a small bowl; reserve remaining pudding mix for the frosting. Prepare the 1/3 cup instant pudding mix with 1 cup milk according to package directions. Refrigerate 10 minutes. Split pound cake lengthwise into 3 layers. Place bottom layer on a serving plate. Spread half the chilled pudding on bottom layer. Top with another cake layer. Spread with remaining pudding. Add remaining cake layer; refrigerate. In a small mixing bowl, mix whipped topping mix, remaining dry instant pudding mix, 1 cup cold milk, and vanilla. Beat with electric mixer on high speed until peaks form, about 5 minutes. Frost cake with whipped topping mixture and sprinkle with pistachio nuts. Store in refrigerator. Makes 8 to 10 servings.

Herbed Macaroni Salad   *Photo on pages 4 and 5.*

Fold the croutons in last so they'll remain crisp.

2 cups shell macaroni, cooked, drained (about 4 cups cooked)	1/2 cup milk
1/2 cup chopped celery	4 oz. process cheese with onion, cubed (1 cup)
1/4 cup chopped green onion	3 hard-cooked eggs, sliced
1/4 cup chopped pimiento	1 cup cheese croutons
1 envelope herb dressing mix with buttermilk	Paprika
1 cup mayonnaise or mayonnaise-style salad dressing	

In a large bowl, mix macaroni, celery, green onion and pimiento; set aside. In a small bowl, mix dressing mix, mayonnaise or salad dressing and milk. Beat with a whisk until smooth. Fold 3/4 cup dressing into macaroni mixture. Cover and refrigerate salad and remaining dressing 3 hours or overnight. Just before serving, fold in cheese, eggs and croutons. Add enough remaining dressing to moisten. Sprinkle with paprika. Makes 8 to 10 servings.

Solo Meal with a Gourmet Touch

Don't throw out that dab of leftover rice! Add a little sautéed celery and onion, some lemon juice and lemon peel to make a delicious stuffed trout. Bacon wrapped around the stuffed fish has two purposes: it holds in the stuffing and keeps the fish moist while it's cooking.

After you turn the fish over, cook the corn on the cob in another skillet. It's so good you may want to cook two ears!

Keep a jar of spiced peaches in the refrigerator to use as a quick garnish that doubles as a salad. And another time, when you're preparing a quick relish tray, the spiced peaches will add something different for color, texture and flavor.

Menu
Rice-Stuffed Trout
Devilish Corn-on-the-Cob
Spiced Peaches
Seeded Hard Roll
Butter
Creme de Menthe Sundae
Coffee

Devilish Corn-on-the-Cob

Try deviled corn-on-the-cob for a change—you'll like it!

1 tablespoon butter or margarine
1/2 teaspoon prepared mustard

1/4 teaspoon celery salt
1 ear corn

Melt butter or margarine in a medium skillet. Stir in mustard and celery salt. Add corn. Cover and cook over medium heat until done, 5 to 6 minutes, turning often. Remove corn with tongs and place on a serving plate. Pour mustard mixture over corn. Makes 1 serving.

1/Spoon lemon-rice filling into a fresh or thawed frozen trout.

2/Wind strips of bacon around trout to add flavor and hold in the stuffing.

How to Make Rice-Stuffed Trout

Rice-Stuffed Trout

Pan-dressed *means the fish is cleaned, scaled and trimmed.*

1 tablespoon butter or margarine
1 tablespoon chopped celery
1 tablespoon chopped onion
1/4 cup cooked rice
1 tablespoon chopped pimiento

2 teaspoons lemon juice
1/4 teaspoon grated lemon peel
1 (5-oz.) trout, pan-dressed
2 slices bacon

Melt butter or margarine in a small skillet. Add celery and onion. Cook and stir over medium heat until tender. Stir in cooked rice, pimiento, lemon juice and lemon peel; toss to mix well. Stuff trout with rice mixture. Wrap bacon around trout and secure with wooden picks. Place fish in a medium skillet. Cook uncovered over medium heat 6 minutes. Turn fish over. Cover and cook 5 minutes. Uncover and, holding fish on edge with tongs, cook 1 to 2 minutes on each edge until bacon is browned and fish flakes easily with a fork. Makes 1 serving.

Variation

To broil fish, preheat broiler to moderate temperature. Place stuffed fish on rack in broiler pan. Broil 5 inches from heat 10 minutes. Turn fish over and broil 6 minutes longer or until fish flakes easily with a fork.

Teenager's Pizza Party

When you're expecting a houseful of teenagers, put popcorn, sausage, fresh vegetables, sour cream dip and apples on your shopping list. They'll enjoy assembling and cooking their own miniature pizzas while nibbling on vegetable dippers and seasoned sour cream.

Handling popcorn that's mixed with hot syrup can cause serious burns. Butter all hands well to protect them from the hot syrup. Rubber gloves are a good idea, but don't forget to butter them to make shaping the popcorn balls easier.

Menu

Miniature Sausage Pizzas
Vegetable Dippers
Sour Cream Dip
Soft Drinks
Peanutty Popcorn Balls
Crisp Apples

Peanutty Popcorn Balls

If you wear rubber gloves to protect your hands from hot syrup, be sure to butter the gloves.

3 cups popped popcorn	**1/2 cup light corn syrup**
1/2 cup salted peanuts	**1/4 cup peanut butter**
1/2 cup packed brown sugar	**1 teaspoon vanilla extract**

Mix popcorn and peanuts in a large bowl; set aside. Combine sugar and corn syrup in a medium saucepan. Cook and stir until brown sugar dissolves and mixture boils. Stir in peanut butter and vanilla until peanut butter melts. Pour over popcorn mixture immediately. Stir to coat popcorn mixture well. With buttered hands, shape mixture into balls. Makes 6 popcorn balls.

1/Roll out refrigerated biscuits to 3-1/2-inch circles. It's easier to transfer circles to a baking sheet at this point than when they contain the toppings.

2/Top each circle with tomato paste, oregano, browned sausage, fennel seeds and cheese, then bake.

How to Make Miniature Sausage Pizzas

Miniature Sausage Pizzas

Teens enjoy fixing—not to mention eating—their own pizzas.

8 oz. bulk pork sausage
1/4 teaspoon garlic powder
1/2 teaspoon ground cumin
1 (3.75-oz.) tube flaky-style refrigerated biscuits (6 biscuits)

2 tablespoons tomato paste
Dried leaf oregano to taste
Fennel seeds to taste
1/2 cup shredded mozzarella cheese

Preheat oven to 400°F (205°C). Crumble sausage into a small skillet. Add garlic powder and cumin. Cook and stir until sausage is browned; drain. On a lightly floured surface, roll out each biscuit to a circle 3-1/2 inches in diameter. Place circles on baking sheet. Spread each circle with 1 teaspoon tomato paste. Sprinkle with oregano. Top with browned sausage, fennel seed and cheese. Bake 12 minutes or until crusts are browned. Makes 6 small pizzas.

Spur-of-the-Moment Company Dinner

Don't let last-minute supper guests put you through a long evening in the kitchen. A fast trip to the store and this dinner will be well underway! Better yet, keep spaghetti dinner mix and cheese sauce mix on hand for such an emergency. You can substitute any leftover meat for the pepperoni, use canned mushrooms and artichokes instead of chopped fresh vegetables, and add canned sliced salad tomatoes for color.

Italian dinner wedges are a quick fix-up for prepared pizza crust and a pleasant change from the usual French bread. Instead of fresh salad greens, toss cooked frozen Italian green beans with vinegar and oil. And if you're lucky enough to live near an Italian bakery, serve one of their marvelous desserts for the finale.

Menu

Shortcut Spaghetti Supper
Romaine Salad
Oil & Vinegar Dressing
Italian Dinner Wedges, page 120
Beer
Spumoni
Packaged Pirouette Cookies
Coffee

Shortcut Spaghetti Supper

Prepare the sauce at the table in your prettiest chafing dish.

1 (8-oz.) pkg. tangy Italian style spaghetti dinner mix (with spaghetti, Parmesan cheese and herb-spice mix)
2 envelopes cheese sauce mix
Milk

3 to 4 oz. sliced pepperoni
1/4 cup sliced green onions
1/4 cup coarsely chopped green pepper
1 tomato, cut in wedges

Cook spaghetti in boiling water according to package directions. Drain spaghetti well and return it to the saucepan. In a medium saucepan, combine both envelopes of cheese sauce mix and herb packet from spaghetti dinner mix. Stir in the milk called for on both packages of cheese sauce mix. Cook sauce according to package directions. Add pepperoni, green onions, green pepper, and tomato wedges to spaghetti. Sprinkle with Parmesan cheese from spaghetti dinner mix; toss gently. Place on a platter. Pour sauce over spaghetti; toss to mix well. Makes 4 servings.

Posh Picnic for Four

Here's a menu that adapts well to any picnic—whether you're celebrating the arrival of spring, Fourth of July or a rousing football victory. Besides being tasty, all the cooking is done long before the big event. Marinate the flank steak in a simple marinade of rum and soy sauce. After broiling or grilling, chill it until just before serving or packing time. Then carefully cut wafer thin slices diagonally across the grain of the meat for maximum tenderness. If the picnic is a stand-up affair, serve the tangy meat slices with tiny party rye bread for easier eating.

Menu

Zesty Tomato Sipper
Peppy Popcorn, page 141
Steak Slices Supreme, page 86
Pumpernickel Bread
Mustard   Pickles
Make-Ahead Salad Toss, page 91
Fresh Fruit Basket
Chocolate Bourbon Balls, page 150
Coffee

Zesty Tomato Sipper

Use a funnel to pour this hot appetizer into a half gallon thermos.

1 (15-oz.) can tomato juice
1 (14-1/2-oz.) can chicken broth
1 (14-1/2-oz.) can beef broth
Dash hot pepper sauce
1/2 teaspoon dried leaf fines herbes

1/4 teaspoon dried leaf marjoram
1/4 teaspoon dried dillweed
1/4 teaspoon dried leaf basil
1/2 bay leaf
Parsley sprigs, if desired

In a large saucepan, mix all ingredients except parsley sprigs. Bring to a boil; reduce heat. Simmer uncovered 15 minutes. Remove bay leaf. Serve in mugs. Top each serving with a parsley sprig, if desired. Makes 5 cups.

Fancy Dinner for Four

Unless your guests have petite appetites, it would be a good idea to double the Beef Wellington Bundles recipe to make 4 bundles. Don't assemble the bundles more than an hour before baking or the crusts will become soggy.

Shape the butter into balls or curls with one of the handy gourmet gadgets that are specially designed for this purpose. It won't take very long and the nicely shaped butter pieces will add style to your table setting.

If butterscotch doesn't appeal to you, make the parfaits with your favorite instant pudding mix and substitute other crushed candies or drained fruit for the brickle chips.

Menu

Beef Wellington Bundles, page 23
Buttered Asparagus Spears
Fancy Tossed Salad, page 95
Butterhorn Rolls   Butter
Champagne
Butterscotch Crunch Parfaits
Coffee

Butterscotch Crunch Parfaits

Evaporated milk makes extra rich and creamy pudding.

1 (3-3/4-oz.) pkg. instant butterscotch pudding mix	Milk or other liquid
1 (13-oz.) can evaporated milk (1-2/3 cups)	1/4 cup almond brickle chips for baking
1 envelope whipped topping mix	1/4 cup toasted flaked coconut
	Toasted flaked coconut for garnish

Prepare butterscotch pudding mix according to package directions, substituting evaporated milk for the liquid called for on the package. Refrigerate while preparing topping but no longer than 5 minutes so pudding mixture will not become firm. Prepare whipped topping mix with milk or other liquid according to package directions. Fold 1/2 cup prepared topping into pudding mixture. Fold almond brickle chips and 1/4 cup toasted coconut into remaining whipped topping. In parfait glasses, alternate layers of pudding mixture and topping mixture. Garnish with additional toasted coconut. Refrigerate until serving time. Makes 3 or 4 servings.

Quick & Easy Dinner for Two

This stew adapts easily to many variations. Try using lamb, pork or chicken strips instead of beef. Or use leftover ham or other leftover meat.

Look through the frozen vegetable section in the supermarket for other frozen mixed international vegetables with flavored sauce cubes. Substitute your favorite vegetable combination for Danish-style vegetables. You can also substitute tomato sauce, hollandaise sauce or another canned gravy for mushroom gravy.

Crisp Cheese-Corn Cakes are as wonderful with soup or salad as they are with stew. Try them another time with hot baked beans and ham cubes spooned on top.

Menu

Danish-Style Stew
Deli Cole Slaw
Cheese-Corn Cakes
Canned Apricots
Chocolate Cookies
Coffee

Cheese-Corn Cakes

The cornmeal flavor goes great with any stew or soup.

1/2 cup cornmeal	**1/2 cup milk**
1/2 cup packaged biscuit mix	**1 tablespoon vegetable oil**
2 tablespoons sugar	**1/2 cup shredded process American cheese**
1 egg	**1 tablespoon butter or margarine**

In a medium bowl, mix cornmeal, biscuit mix and sugar. Make a well in the center. Add egg, milk and oil to well. Stir until just combined. Fold in cheese. Melt butter or margarine on a griddle. Using 2 tablespoons batter for each cake, cook cakes over medium-high heat until browned, about 1-1/2 minutes on each side. Makes 8 cakes.

1/After cooking steak strips, stir together thawed vegetables, gravy, Worcestershire sauce and wine.

2/Heat vegetable mixture until vegetables are tender. Add steak strips. Heat through before serving.

How to Make Danish-Style Stew

Danish-Style Stew

This version is Danish but any mixed vegetable with sauce cubes can be used.

2 tablespoons butter or margarine
8 oz. beef sirloin, cut in strips
  1/4 inch thick
1 (10-oz.) pkg. frozen Danish-style
  vegetables, thawed

1/2 cup canned mushroom gravy
1 tablespoon Burgundy wine
1 teaspoon Worcestershire sauce

Melt butter or margarine in a medium skillet. Add steak strips. Cook and stir until done as desired. Remove steak strips and keep warm, reserving drippings in skillet. In a medium bowl, mix vegetables, gravy, Burgundy and Worcestershire sauce. Add to drippings in skillet. Cook and stir until vegetables are tender. Stir in steak strips; heat through. Makes 2 servings.

Candlelight Dinner for Two

Brandy needs to be warm if you plan to ignite it. Be sure to use a long-handled match and be quick!

If you are preparing the steaks or dessert in a chafing dish, cook over the direct flame, not over the *bain marie* (the part that holds water under the skillet). Both sauces need the heat of a direct flame to thicken. Another time substitute peaches for the cherries and serve over scoops of pecans praline ice cream.

Menu

Steak Diane Flambé
Boston Lettuce
Tomato Wedges
Avocado Slices
Clear French Dressing
Croissants   Butter
Burgundy
Cherries Jubilee
Coffee

Cherries Jubilee

What could be more impressive than the flaming entree? A flaming dessert!

1 (16-oz.) can pitted dark sweet cherries
Water, if necessary
1/4 cup sugar
1 tablespoon cornstarch

1 teaspoon lemon juice
3 tablespoons warm brandy
Vanilla ice cream

Drain cherries; reserve syrup. If necessary, add water to syrup to make 3/4 cup. In a small saucepan, mix sugar and cornstarch. Gradually stir in syrup. Cook and stir until thickened and bubbly. Stir in cherries and lemon juice. Ignite brandy. Pour flaming brandy into sauce. Serve over ice cream when flame subsides. Makes 2 servings.

Spoon brandy-spiked mushroom sauce over steaks just before serving.

When the flame subsides, ladle brandied cherry sauce over vanilla ice cream.

How to Make Steak Diane Flambé and Cherries Jubilee

Steak Diane Flambé

Set your chafing dish on the table and get ready for a dramatic dinner.

2 tablespoons butter or margarine
2 (8-oz.) beef rib eye steaks
1/2 cup fresh mushroom slices
1/4 cup chopped onion
1 garlic clove, minced

1/3 cup ketchup
1/2 teaspoon prepared mustard
1/2 teaspoon Worcestershire sauce
2 tablespoons warm brandy

Melt butter or margarine in a medium skillet. Add steaks. Cook until browned, 3 to 5 minutes. Turn and cook until done as desired, 4 to 5 minutes for rare. Remove steaks and keep warm. Add mushrooms, onion and garlic to skillet. Cook and stir until heated through. Stir in ketchup, mustard and Worcestershire sauce. Cook and stir until heated through. Ignite brandy. Stir flaming brandy into sauce. Flame will gradually go out. Spoon sauce over steaks. Makes 2 servings.

Simple Suppers

Sometimes the easiest way to approach a meal is to decide how it will be cooked. On a cool night, use your oven for a hot baked dish such as Beef Wellington Bundles or Zesty Baked Fish. If time is short because you have something special to do after supper, a quick skillet meal is the answer. Try Jiffy Beef Stroganoff or Pineapple Ham Loaf.

With a little extra time in the morning, you can do some advance preparation for supper. Pour a quick marinade over rib-eye steaks. Let them marinate all day in the refrigerator and you'll be able to prepare Steak de Burgo while you're setting the table!

Before you make a decision about tonight's supper, take a look at a few ideas that can make supper a truly simple—but delicious—affair.
• Marinate steaks, chops or chicken breasts in a mixture of Italian salad dressing, dry sherry and a dash of Worcestershire sauce. Broil or grill the delightfully flavored meats over barbecue coals.
• Broil or pan-grill a thick fully cooked slice of ham. Top with heated canned peaches or pineapple, frozen creamed peas and potatoes, or heated cranberry-orange relish.
• Sauté veal cutlets in butter. Stir in some sliced fresh or canned mushrooms, a dash of garlic salt and a splash of lemon juice.
• Thread steak cubes on skewers with vegetables and cook them on your outdoor grill or in your broiler. You can also cook steak cubes in hot oil at the table for fondue or simmer them in a full-bodied broth with vegetables for stew.
• Stir-fry thin strips of pork or chicken. Toss in a cup or two of sliced fresh vegetables such as celery, green pepper, carrots, green onion, cherry tomatoes, spinach and a sprinkling of bean sprouts. Stir-fry until the vegetables are crisp-tender then season with ginger and soy sauce.
• Dredge chicken pieces in a packaged coating mix. After baking, stir a can of cream of chicken soup and some milk into the pan drippings. Add a little poultry seasoning. Serve the gravy over instant mashed potatoes with the oven-fried chicken.

Beef Wellington Bundles

No one said it could be easy—until now!

8 oz. ground beef	1 (3-oz.) can sliced mushrooms, drained
Garlic salt	Garlic salt
1 tablespoon butter or margarine	Snipped chives
1 tablespoon brandy	Dash pepper
2 frozen patty shells, thawed	1 (1-oz.) slice braunschweiger, halved

Preheat oven to 450°F (230°C). Shape beef into 2 patties about 3 inches in diameter. Sprinkle with garlic salt. Melt butter or margarine in a medium skillet. When butter sizzles, add patties. Cook over medium-high heat 2 minutes. Turn patties and drizzle with brandy. Cook 1 minute longer. Remove from pan. On a lightly floured surface, roll out each patty shell to a 7-inch square. Pat mushrooms dry on paper towels. Spoon mushrooms onto center of each pastry square; sprinkle with garlic salt, chives and pepper. Place braunschweiger, then patties on mushrooms. Fold dough over patties. Moisten edges and press with your fingertips to seal. Place bundles on a baking sheet. Place in oven and reduce oven temperature to 400°F (205°C). Bake 20 to 22 minutes or until golden brown. Makes 2 servings.

How to Make Beef Wellington Bundles

1/Roll out patty shells to 7-inch squares. Spoon mushrooms onto center of square. Sprinkle with garlic salt, chives and pepper.

2/Place a slice of braunschweiger then a cooked hamburger patty on mushrooms. Fold dough up over patties, moisten edges and seal before baking.

Steak de Burgo

Burgundy wine and herbs enhance rib eye steak.

1 cup Burgundy wine
1 tablespoon Worcestershire sauce
1/2 teaspoon dried leaf basil
1/2 tcaspoon dried leaf thyme
1/4 teaspoon dry mustard

Dash garlic powder
2 (8-oz.) beef rib eye steaks
1/4 cup butter or margarine
4 frozen French-fried onion rings
1/2 cup fresh mushroom slices

In a small bowl, mix Burgundy, Worcestershire sauce, basil, thyme, mustard and garlic powder. Place steaks in a heavy plastic bag. Place plastic bag in a shallow baking pan. Pour marinade into bag; seal bag. Marinate in refrigerator 8 hours or overnight, turning bag over occasionally. Melt butter or margarine in a large skillet. Add onion rings. Cook over medium-high heat until golden brown. Remove onion rings and keep warm; reserve butter or margarine in skillet. Drain steak; reserve 1/2 cup marinade. Cook steaks in butter or margarine in skillet until done as desired, turning several times. Place steaks on a platter; reserve drippings in skillet. Cook and stir mushrooms in drippings until barely tender. Stir in reserved marinade. Cook and stir until heated through. Pour over steaks. Top with cooked onion rings. Makes 2 servings.

Mushroom-Smothered Strip Steak

What could be more appetizing than a juicy steak covered with mushrooms?

2 tablespoons butter or margarine
2 (8-oz.) New York strip steaks
Salt and pepper

1 tablespoon butter or margarine
1 cup fresh mushroom slices

Melt 2 tablespoons butter or margarine in a large skillet. Add steaks. Cook over medium heat until done as desired, turning several times. Place steaks on a platter and keep warm. Season to taste with salt and pepper. Melt 1 tablespoon butter or margarine in skillet. Add mushrooms. Cook and stir until tender, about 2 minutes. Spoon on top of steaks. Makes 2 servings.

Jiffy Beef Stroganoff

Rich and creamy stroganoff becomes a true delicacy when it's served over wild rice.

Wild rice
Water
Salt
2 tablespoons butter or margarine
8 oz. beef sirloin steak, cut in
  1/4-inch strips
1/2 cup fresh mushroom slices

2 tablespoons chopped onion
Garlic salt
1/3 cup beef broth
1 tablespoon all-purpose flour
1 tablespoon ketchup
1/2 cup dairy sour cream

Prepare wild rice with water and salt according to package directions; keep warm. Melt butter or margarine in a medium skillet. Add steak strips, mushrooms and onion. Cook and stir over medium-high heat until steak strips are almost done as desired. Sprinkle with garlic salt. In a small bowl, mix broth, flour and ketchup. Stir into steak strips. Cook and stir until thickened and bubbly. Remove from heat. Stir a small amount of hot sauce into sour cream. Stir mixture into skillet. Heat through; do not boil. Serve immediately over wild rice. Makes 2 servings.

Sirloin Tip Roquefort

Blue cheese salad dressing adds brisk flavor to sliced sirloin rolls.

1 tablespoon vegetable oil
2 (3-oz.) thin slices beef sirloin tip
Salt and pepper
2 tablespoons blue cheese salad dressing

Boston lettuce leaves
Cherry tomatoes
Crumbled Roquefort or blue cheese

Heat oil in a large skillet. Cook sirloin tip slices over medium-high heat in oil until browned; turn and cook until done as desired. Season with salt and pepper. Spread cooked sirloin tip slices with dressing. Roll up and secure with wooden picks. Serve on lettuce leaves. Garnish with cherry tomatoes and crumbled cheese. Makes 2 servings.

Gourmet Beef & Macaroni

Mushrooms and seasonings turn ground beef and macaroni and cheese into a gourmet's delight.

8 oz. ground beef
1 (2-1/2-oz.) can sliced mushrooms, drained
3 tablespoons chopped pimiento
1/4 teaspoon dried leaf thyme
1 (12-oz.) pkg. frozen macaroni and
  cheese, thawed

4 slices tomato
Seasoned salt
Snipped fresh parsley

In a large skillet, cook and stir ground beef over medium-high heat until lightly browned. Drain off excess fat. Stir in mushrooms, pimiento and thyme. Reduce heat to medium-low. Add macaroni. Cook until heated through, stirring frequently. Place tomato slices on top of macaroni. Cover and cook until heated. Sprinkle with seasoned salt and parsley. Makes 3 servings.

Minute Steaks Greek-Style

Wonderful flavor from yogurt, herbs and a medley of vegetables.

4 tablespoons butter or margarine	4 beef cubed steaks, 1/4 inch thick (1 lb.)
1 small onion, sliced, separated in rings	Garlic salt
1 small green pepper, cut in strips	1 tablespoon all-purpose flour
Salt and pepper	1 (8-oz.) carton plain yogurt (1 cup)
1 teaspoon dried leaf oregano	1 small cucumber, peeled, seeded, grated
1 tomato, cut in wedges	(1/2 cup)
1 tablespoon butter or margarine	1/4 teaspoon garlic salt

In a large skillet, melt 4 tablespoons butter or margarine. Add onion and green pepper. Season with salt, pepper and oregano. Cook and stir until onion is almost tender. Add tomato wedges; heat through. Place vegetables on a platter and keep warm. Melt 1 tablespoon butter or margarine in skillet. Cook steaks quickly on both sides 5 or 6 minutes for rare, turning once. Season with garlic salt. Place steaks on platter with vegetables and keep warm. Stir flour into yogurt, then stir several tablespoons of the hot pan juices into yogurt mixture. Stir yogurt, cucumber and 1/4 teaspoon garlic salt into skillet. Heat through, stirring often; do not boil. Spoon a little yogurt sauce over steaks and vegetables. Serve remaining yogurt sauce separately. Makes 4 servings.

Chinese Pepper Steak

Serve over rice to temper the exotic Eastern flavor.

2 tablespoons vegetable oil	1/2 cup beef broth
1 green pepper, cut in strips	1 tablespoon soy sauce
8 oz. beef sirloin steak, cut in	1 tablespoon dry sherry
1" x 1/8" strips	1 garlic clove, minced
1 tablespoon cold water	1/4 teaspoon grated fresh ginger root
2 teaspoons cornstarch	

Heat oil in a medium skillet. Cook and stir green pepper in oil until crisp-tender. Remove and keep warm. Add steak strips to skillet. Cook and stir until browned. Add browned steak strips to green pepper; reserve drippings in skillet. Keep steak and green pepper mixture warm. Mix water and cornstarch in a small bowl; set aside. Stir broth, soy sauce, sherry, garlic and ginger root into drippings in skillet. Add cornstarch mixture. Cook and stir until mixture is thickened and bubbly, about 3 minutes. Stir in green pepper and steak. Serve at once. Makes 2 servings.

Swiss Steak Supper

A good money-saving recipe.

8 oz. beef chuck steak, 1/2 inch thick
Unseasoned instant meat tenderizer
1/2 cup all-purpose flour
1/2 teaspoon salt
1/8 teaspoon pepper
2 tablespoons vegetable oil
1 small onion, sliced, separated in rings

1 tablespoon cornstarch
1 cup beef broth
2 tablespoons chili sauce
2 teaspoons brown sugar
1 teaspoon Worcestershire sauce
1 garlic clove, minced

Use a meat mallet to pound steak 1/4 inch thick. Cut steak in half crosswise. Use meat tenderizer according to package directions. Combine flour, salt and pepper in a plastic bag. Shake steak in bag until evenly coated with flour mixture. Heat oil in a large skillet. Cook steak in oil until browned. Turn and cook until done as desired. Keep warm on a platter; reserve drippings in skillet. Cook and stir onion in drippings until tender. Stir cornstarch into onion. Add broth, chili sauce, brown sugar, Worcestershire sauce and garlic. Cook and stir until mixture is thickened and bubbly. Spoon over steaks. Makes 2 servings.

Calves Liver Combo

Cook liver a little on the rare side. Overcooked liver is tough and dry.

3 slices bacon
1/2 onion, sliced, separated in rings
1/2 cup all-purpose flour
1/2 teaspoon salt
1/8 teaspoon pepper

8 oz. calves liver
2 tablespoons vegetable oil
1 teaspoon all-purpose flour
1/2 cup beef broth

Cook bacon in a medium skillet until crisp. Crumble and set aside; reserve drippings in skillet. Cook onion in drippings until tender. Add to bacon. In a pie plate, mix 1/2 cup flour, salt and pepper. Dredge liver in flour mixture. Heat oil in skillet. Cook and turn liver in oil until done, about 5 minutes. Remove and keep warm. Stir 1 teaspoon flour into drippings in skillet. Stir in broth, crumbled bacon and cooked onion. Cook and stir until mixture is thickened and bubbly, about 2 minutes. Spoon over liver. Makes 2 servings.

Swedish-Style Meatballs

Hearty meatballs in savory gravy are perfect over egg noodles.

1 egg	4 oz. ground pork
1/4 cup quick-cooking oats	2 tablespoons butter or margarine
1/4 cup chopped onion	2 tablespoons all-purpose flour
1/4 cup milk	1 teaspoon instant beef bouillon granules
1/2 teaspoon salt	1/8 teaspoon ground nutmeg
1/8 teaspoon ground nutmeg	1 cup milk
1/8 teaspoon pepper	Salt and pepper
4 oz. ground beef	Hot cooked noodles

In a medium bowl, whisk egg, oatmeal, onion, 1/4 cup milk, salt, 1/8 teaspoon nutmeg and 1/8 teaspoon pepper. Add beef and pork; mix well. If desired, chill mixture for easier shaping. Shape into twelve 1-inch balls. Melt butter or margarine in a medium skillet. Add meatballs. Cook over medium-high heat, turning frequently until done as desired. Remove and keep warm; reserve drippings in skillet. Stir flour, bouillon granules and 1/8 teaspoon nutmeg into drippings. Add 1 cup milk. Cook and stir until gravy is thickened and bubbly. Season with salt and pepper. Pour gravy over meatballs. Serve over hot cooked noodles. Makes 2 or 3 servings.

Variations

To bake meatballs, preheat oven to 375°F (190°C). Place meatballs in a baking dish and bake 20 to 25 minutes.
For an easy make-ahead dinner, freeze meatballs uncooked and bake 30 to 35 minutes.

How to Make Swedish-Style Meatballs

It's easier to shape meatballs if the meat mixture is chilled first. The meat mixture will stick to your hands less if your hands are wet.

Fast Meatball Suppers

- Prepare 2 packages of cheese sauce mix according to package directions. Add a little Worcestershire sauce and dry mustard. Stir in cooked meatballs. Serve over frozen or packaged white and wild rice.

- Heat canned spaghetti sauce. Stir in cooked meatballs and serve sauce and meatballs over green noodles. Top each serving with Parmesan cheese.

- Prepare 2 packages of Stroganoff sauce mix according to package directions. Stir in cooked meatballs and a can of sliced mushrooms. Serve over mounds of instant mashed potatoes.

Chunky Chili with Cheese

To make extra-juicy chili, stir in 1/4 cup of tomato juice.

8 oz. ground beef
1 (8-oz.) can red kidney beans, drained
1 (8-oz.) can tomatoes, chopped
1 tablespoon dried minced onion flakes

1 teaspoon garlic salt
1 teaspoon chili powder
4 oz. process American cheese, cut in
   1/2-inch cubes (1 cup)

In a medium skillet, cook and stir ground beef until no longer pink. Drain off excess fat. Add beans, tomatoes, onion flakes, garlic salt and chili powder to cooked beef. Cook and stir until heated through. Remove from heat. Stir in cheese. Makes 2 servings.

Pork Chops with Apple Stuffing

Succulent chops with an unusual apple-raisin-bread stuffing.

1 tablespoon vegetable oil
2 (4-oz.) pork loin chops, 1/2 inch thick
1/4 cup chopped apple
1/4 cup chopped celery

3 slices raisin bread, cubed
3 tablespoons apple juice
Dash ground nutmeg

Heat oil in a medium skillet. Cook pork chops in oil over medium heat until lightly browned on both sides. Continue to cook until browned well and meat is no longer pink when cut. Remove chops from skillet and keep warm; reserve 2 tablespoons drippings in skillet. Cook and stir apple and celery in drippings until tender. Add raisin bread, apple juice and nutmeg. Cook and stir until heated through. Serve with pork chops. Makes 2 servings.

Smoked Pork Chops Cassis

Creme de cassis is a sweet liqueur made from black currants.

1/4 cup black currant jelly
1 tablespoon creme de cassis
1 tablespoon vegetable oil

2 (4-oz.) fully cooked smoked pork chops,
   1/2 inch thick

In a small bowl, mix jelly and creme de cassis; set aside. Heat oil in a medium skillet. Cook pork chops in oil over medium heat until lightly browned. Turn, spoon glaze on chops, and cook until other side is lightly browned and chops are heated through. Spoon glaze over chops several times to prevent glaze from burning. Makes 2 servings.

Brandied Fruit Pork Chops

Fruit and brandy add elegance to grilled pork chops.

1 tablespoon vegetable oil
2 (6-oz.) pork loin chops, 1/2 inch thick
Salt and pepper
1/3 cup peach slices
1/3 cup pineapple chunks

1/3 cup orange marmalade
1 tablespoon brandy
2 slices orange
2 slices lime
2 maraschino cherries, if desired

Heat oil in a medium skillet. Cook pork chops in oil over medium heat until lightly browned. Turn and cook until browned well and meat is no longer pink when cut. Season with salt and pepper. Remove and keep warm. Drain drippings from skillet. Combine peaches, pineapple, marmalade and brandy in skillet. Cook and stir until heated through. Spoon over chops. Top with orange slices, lime slices and maraschino cherries, if desired. Makes 2 servings.

Pork Wild Rice Supper

Thaw rice quickly under running water while vegetables and pork are cooking.

2 tablespoons vegetable oil
1 (2-1/2-oz.) can mushrooms, drained
3 tablespoons chopped green onion
2 (4-oz.) pork tenderloins, cut in
  1-inch strips

1 (11-oz.) pkg. frozen long-grain and
  wild rice, thawed
1 tomato, cubed

Heat oil in a medium skillet over medium heat. Cook mushrooms, onion and pork in oil until pork is no longer pink, stirring often. Add rice and tomato to pork mixture. Cook until heated through, stirring gently. Makes 3 servings.

Hot Reuben Salad

All the tantalizing flavors of a Reuben sandwich in a hot salad.

1 tablespoon butter or margarine
1 tablespoon chopped celery
1 tablespoon chopped onion
1 tablespoon chopped green pepper
1 (8-oz.) can sauerkraut, drained and rinsed

4 oz. corned beef, cut in strips
1 tablespoon chopped pimiento
1/4 cup Thousand Island dressing
1/2 cup shredded Swiss cheese
2 rye rolls, if desired

In a medium skillet, melt butter or margarine. Add celery, onion and green pepper. Cook and stir until tender. Stir in sauerkraut, corned beef, pimiento and dressing. Cook and stir until heated through. Top with shredded cheese. Serve with rye rolls, if desired. Makes 2 servings.

Veal Scallopini

If veal sirloin steaks are not available, use veal loin or rib chops, round steaks or shoulder steaks.

2 (4-oz.) boneless veal sirloin steaks
Salt and pepper
2 tablespoons butter or margarine
1/2 cup chopped onion

1/2 cup chopped fresh mushrooms
1/4 cup beef broth
1 tablespoon dry sherry

Use a meat mallet to pound veal 1/8 inch thick. Sprinkle with salt and pepper. Melt butter or margarine in a medium skillet. Add onion and mushrooms. Cook and stir over medium-high heat until tender. Place on a platter and keep warm. Cook veal in skillet until browned and done as desired, turning once. Add to onion and mushrooms on platter; keep warm. Cook and stir broth and sherry in skillet until heated. Spoon over vegetables and veal. Makes 2 servings.

Quick Veal Parmigiana

Almost as soon as you feel a craving for Italian food, this meal can be on the table.

2 (4-oz.) veal sirloin steaks
3/4 cup seasoned breadcrumbs
1/4 cup grated Parmesan cheese
1 egg, beaten

1/4 cup vegetable oil
1 cup bottled Italian cooking sauce
1/4 cup shredded mozzarella cheese

Use a meat mallet to pound veal 1/8 inch thick. In a pie plate, mix breadcrumbs and Parmesan cheese. Dip veal in breadcrumb mixture, then in egg, then again in crumb mixture. Heat oil in a medium skillet. Cook breaded veal in hot oil over medium heat until browned and done as desired, turning once. Place on a platter and keep warm. Drain drippings from skillet. Cook and stir Italian sauce in skillet until heated through. Spoon over veal and sprinkle with mozzarella cheese. Makes 2 servings.

Veal Cordon Bleu a la Ascona

A delicious variation of the popular classic—ham and Swiss cheese between tender veal slices.

2 (4-oz.) veal sirloin steaks
2 slices cooked ham
2 slices Swiss cheese
Dash ground sage

2 tablespoons butter or margarine
1 cup fresh mushroom slices
1/4 cup dry white wine

Use a meat mallet to pound veal steaks 1/8 inch thick. Cut in half crosswise. Place a ham slice, then a cheese slice on 2 of the halves. Sprinkle with sage. Top with second veal steak halves. Pound edges to seal. Melt butter or margarine in a medium skillet. Cook veal over medium heat until browned and done as desired, turning carefully once. Place on a platter; reserve drippings in skillet. Cook and stir mushrooms in drippings until tender. Stir in wine. Cook and stir until heated through. Spoon over veal. Makes 2 servings.

How to Make Veal Cordon Bleu a la Ascona

1/Pound veal until it is 1/8 inch thick. Halve crosswise. Top 1 half with a slice of ham and a slice of cheese.

2/Place the other half of veal over the ham and cheese, then pound the edges to seal.

Ham Yam Logs

Everyone will enjoy these ham roll-ups filled with sweet potato and fruit.

1 (8-oz.) can sweet potatoes, drained, cut up
1 medium banana, sliced
1/4 cup pineapple preserves
4 large thin slices cooked ham

Brown sugar
Ground cinnamon
1 tablespoon butter or margarine
Cranberry-orange relish

In a medium bowl, gently mix sweet potatoes, banana and pineapple preserves; do not mash. Spoon mixture onto ham slices. Sprinkle with brown sugar and cinnamon. Roll up and secure with wooden picks. Melt butter or margarine in a large skillet. Add roll-ups. Cook over medium-low heat until heated through, turning often. Garnish with relish. Makes 4 servings.

Pineapple Ham Loaf

Ham and pork loaf with a tropical glaze.

8 oz. ground ham
4 oz. ground pork
1 egg, beaten
1 teaspoon instant minced onion

1/4 cup quick-cooking oats
1/4 cup ketchup
Vegetable oil
Pineapple Glaze, see below

Pineapple Glaze:
1 tablespoon butter or margarine
2 tablespoons brown sugar

2 canned pineapple slices, halved

In a medium bowl, mix ham, pork, egg, onion, oats and ketchup; mix well. Generously brush a 6-1/2- or 7-inch heavy skillet with oil. Pat ham mixture into skillet. Cook over medium-high heat about 6 minutes or until browned well. Loosen edges of loaf with a spatula. Invert loaf onto a plate. Ease loaf back into skillet, reshaping if necessary. Reduce heat to medium. Cover and cook 15 to 20 minutes or until browned. To remove loaf from skillet, loosen edges with a spatula; place the plate on top of loaf and invert. Prepare Pineapple Glaze. Spoon glaze over ham loaf. Cut into wedges. Makes 4 servings.

Pineapple Glaze:
Melt butter or margarine in a small skillet. Stir in brown sugar. Add pineapple. Cook until heated through. Makes about 1/4 cup of glaze.

German-Style Hot Sausage

Drain cooked bacon on paper towels until it crumbles easily.

3 slices bacon
8 oz. fully cooked smoked sausage,
 cut in 1-inch pieces
1/4 cup chopped onion
1/4 cup chopped green pepper
1 tablespoon all-purpose flour
1 tablespoon sugar

1/2 teaspoon dry mustard
1/2 teaspoon celery seed
1/2 teaspoon salt
1/2 cup water
1/4 cup cider vinegar
1 (8-oz.) can whole potatoes, drained,
 sliced

Cook bacon in a large skillet until crisp. Drain; reserve drippings in skillet. Crumble bacon and set aside. Add sausage pieces to drippings in skillet. Cook until heated through and browned, turning often. Remove sausage pieces from skillet and keep warm; reserve drippings in skillet. Cook and stir onion and green pepper in drippings until tender. Stir in flour, sugar, dry mustard, celery seed and salt. Add water and vinegar. Cook and stir until mixture is thickened and bubbly. Stir in potatoes. Cook and stir until heated through. Add sausage. Top each serving with crumbled bacon. Makes 2 or 3 servings.

Chuck Wagon Supper

Great served in tin plates around a campfire or at your own table.

3 slices bacon
3 frankfurters, cut in 1-inch pieces
1 (8-oz.) can pork and beans
2 tablespoons chopped onion

2 tablespoons ketchup
2 teaspoons brown sugar
2 teaspoons prepared mustard

Cook bacon in a medium skillet until crisp. Drain; reserve drippings in skillet. Crumble bacon and set aside. Add frankfurter pieces to drippings in skillet. Cook and turn until browned. Stir in pork and beans, onion, ketchup, brown sugar, mustard and crumbled bacon. Cook and stir until heated through. Makes 2 servings.

Quick Shrimp Newburg

Convenience foods can shorten the preparation of this gourmet meal from hours to minutes.

2 tablespoons butter or margarine
8-oz. cooked shrimp, peeled, deveined
2 tablespoons chopped green onion
2 tablespoons chopped celery
Dash garlic powder

1 (10-oz.) pkg. frozen Welsh rarebit, thawed
2 tablespoons dry sherry
2 or 3 baked patty shells
2 tablespoons grated Parmesan cheese
Snipped fresh dillweed

Melt butter or margarine in a medium skillet. Add shrimp, onion and celery. Cook and stir over medium heat until shrimp is heated through and vegetables are tender. Sprinkle with garlic powder. Stir rarebit and sherry into shrimp mixture. Cook and stir until heated through. Spoon into patty shells. Sprinkle with parmesan cheese and dillweed. Makes 2 or 3 servings.

Zesty Baked Fish

The flavor secret is lemon-butter and a fabulous tartar sauce.

2 frozen fried breaded fish portions
1 tablespoon butter or margarine, melted

1-1/2 teaspoons lemon juice
Tartar Sauce, see below

Tartar Sauce:
2 tablespoons plain yogurt
2 tablespoons mayonnaise or
  mayonnaise-style salad dressing
2 tablespoons sliced stuffed green olives

2 tablespoons chopped dill pickle
Dash salt and pepper
1 hard-cooked egg, chopped

Place fish portions in greased shallow baking pan. Preheat oven to 450°F (230°C). Combine butter or margarine and lemon juice. Drizzle over fish. Bake 15 minutes. Prepare Tartar Sauce. Top fish portions with a spoonful of sauce. Bake 3 minutes longer or until sauce is heated through. Makes 2 servings.

Tartar Sauce:
In a medium bowl, combine yogurt, mayonnaise or salad dressing, olives, pickle, salt and pepper; mix well. Fold in hard-cooked egg. Makes about 2/3 cup of sauce.

Tuna Currywiches

Serve these cold topped with chutney, or top them with cheese, then broil to melt the cheese.

1 (7-oz.) can water pack tuna, drained,
  broken in large chunks
1/2 cup diced unpeeled apple
1/4 cup chopped celery
1 tablespoon chopped green onion
1 tablespoon raisins
1/4 cup mayonnaise or mayonnaise-style
  salad dressing

1-1/2 teaspoons lemon juice
1/4 teaspoon curry powder
Leaf lettuce
2 English muffins, split, toasted
Chutney

In a medium bowl, combine tuna, apple, celery, green onion and raisins. In a small bowl, combine mayonnaise or salad dressing, lemon juice, and curry powder; mix well. Add to tuna mixture; toss gently. Place lettuce on English muffins. Top with generous spoonfuls of tuna mixture; garnish with a spoonful of chutney. Makes 4 servings.

Variation

Omit lettuce and chutney. Broil tuna on English muffins in preheated broiler 1 minute. Halve 2 American cheese slices diagonally. Top each sandwich with a cheese triangle. Broil 1 to 2 minutes longer until cheese melts.

Grilled Turkey Birds

Stuff slices of turkey with sausage and spinach dressing.

4 oz. bulk pork sausage
1 tablespoon chopped onion
1/2 (8-oz.) can spinach, drained, chopped
1/4 cup herb-seasoned breadcrumbs for
  stuffing

1 tablespoon grated Parmesan cheese
4 large thin slices cooked turkey
2 tablespoons butter or margarine
1/2 teaspoon dried rubbed sage

In a medium skillet, cook and stir sausage and onion until sausage is browned. Drain off excess fat. Stir in spinach, breadcrumbs and Parmesan cheese. Cook and stir until heated through. Spoon sausage stuffing onto turkey slices. Roll up and secure with wooden picks. Melt butter or margarine in skillet. Stir in sage. Add turkey roll-ups. Cook until heated through, turning occasionally. Makes 4 servings.

Chicken Véronique

Fresh green grapes and dry white wine enhance chicken breasts sautéed in lemon and butter.

1/2 lemon
2 (4-oz.) chicken breasts, skinned,
   boned, halved
Salt and pepper
2 tablespoons butter or margarine

1 tablespoon cold water
1 teaspoon cornstarch
1/2 cup seedless green grapes
1/3 cup light cream
1 tablespoon dry white wine

Squeeze lemon juice over chicken. Sprinkle with salt and pepper. Melt butter or margarine in a large skillet. Add chicken breasts. Cook until browned and juices run clear when chicken is pierced with a fork, turning as needed. Remove and keep warm; reserve drippings in skillet. Mix water and cornstarch in a small bowl. Stir into drippings. Add grapes and cream. Cook and stir until sauce thickens. Stir in wine. Spoon sauce over chicken. Makes 2 servings.

How to Make Chicken Véronique

1/Remove bone and skin from 2 chicken breasts. Squeeze lemon juice over chicken and sprinkle with salt and pepper.

2/Cook chicken in butter or margarine until tender. Top with a creamy wine and green grape sauce.

Zeus' Lamb Steaks

Greek-style lamb—food for the gods!

2 (8-oz.) lamb blade steaks, 1/2 inch thick
Garlic salt
Dried leaf oregano
Dried leaf basil

Pepper
1 tablespoon olive oil
2 lemon wedges

Sprinkle lamb to taste with garlic salt, oregano, basil and pepper. Heat olive oil in a medium skillet. Cook lamb in oil over medium-high heat until browned and done as desired. Serve with lemon wedges. Makes 2 servings.

Cacciatore Chicken Breasts

Cacciatore *means* hunter's style—*simmered in wine with onions, tomatoes, garlic and herbs.*

2 tablespoons olive oil
1/2 onion, sliced, separated in rings
1/2 green pepper, sliced
2 chicken breasts, skinned, boned, halved
1 (8-oz.) can stewed tomatoes

2 tablespoons dry white wine
1/2 teaspoon garlic salt
1/4 teaspoon dried rosemary
1/8 teaspoon pepper

Heat olive oil in a large skillet. Cook and stir onion and green pepper in olive oil until tender. Remove and keep warm. Cook chicken in skillet until browned and juices run clear when chicken is pierced with a fork; turn once halfway through cooking time. Remove and keep warm. Combine tomatoes, wine, garlic salt, rosemary and pepper in skillet. Cook and stir until heated through. Stir in cooked onion and green pepper. Serve over chicken. Makes 2 servings.

Hot Garbanzo Chicken Salad

You may know garbanzo beans by another name—chick peas.

3 slices bacon
1/4 cup slivered almonds
1 (15-oz.) can garbanzo beans, drained, rinsed
1 (5-oz.) can boned chicken

1/4 cup chopped green onion
2 tablespoons chopped pimiento
1/4 cup Italian salad dressing
2 oz. Monterey Jack cheese, cut in 1/2-inch cubes (1/2 cup)

Cook bacon in a medium skillet until crisp. Drain; reserve drippings in skillet. Crumble bacon and set aside. Cook almonds in drippings until toasted, stirring frequently. Add toasted almonds to bacon; reserve drippings in skillet. Add garbanzo beans, chicken, onion, pimiento and salad dressing to drippings. Cook and stir until heated through. Add cheese cubes, crumbled bacon and almonds; toss gently. Serve at once. Makes 4 servings.

Easy Chicken a la King

You can make this at a moment's notice.

2 tablespoons butter or margarine
1 (5-oz.) can boned chicken
1 (2-1/2-oz.) can mushrooms, drained
1 (10-1/4-oz.) can condensed cream of mushroom soup

1/4 cup milk
2 tablespoons chopped pimiento
2 tablespoons dry white wine
2 English muffins, halved

Melt butter or margarine in a medium saucepan. Add chicken and mushrooms. Cook and stir over medium heat until heated through. In a medium bowl, combine soup, milk, pimiento and wine. Add to chicken mixture. Cook and stir until heated through. Serve over English muffin halves. Makes 4 servings.

Quick Frank & Burger Suppers

Recipes in this section were tested on an electric range, starting with a cold skillet and a cold cooking unit. If you're using a gas range, cooking time will be shorter than the times in the recipes. Food will cook faster if it's in a skillet with a thin bottom or if you preheat the skillet. If food is cooking too fast, reduce the heat.

Store meat in the coldest part of your refrigerator. The temperature should be from 35° to 40°F (0° to 3°C). Many refrigerators have special compartments for meat storage. But don't cram in too much meat! Air should circulate around each package. Prepacked ground meats and frankfurters can be refrigerated in their original wrappings. Use ground meats within 1 to 2 days and frankfurters within 4 to 5 days. Freeze meat wrapped in aluminum foil, heavy-duty clear polyethylene wrap, heavy-duty plastic bags or specially coated freezer paper to seal air out and lock moisture in. Frozen ground beef, veal and lamb will maintain their quality for 3 to 4 months. Frozen ground pork should be used within 1 to 3 months; frozen frankfurters should be used within 1 month.

On a short-notice cookout, picnic or for a fast supper, you may not have time to refer to a recipe. In that case, here are a few ideas to help you add a fast creative touch:

- Use different kinds of buns—whole wheat, rye or seeded. Warm the buns wrapped in foil or grill them beside the meat during the last few minutes of cooking time. Try pita bread, also called *pocket bread*, instead of buns.
- Create your own relish by mixing chopped pickles, olives, onion, tomatoes, and hot or sweet peppers. Stir in mustard and chili sauce to taste.
- Stuff slits in frankfurters with shredded cheese, chopped vegetables, bean sprouts, relish, crushed chips, croutons or herbs. Or sandwich the filling between two thin burger patties. Wrap the franks or burgers with bacon to hold in the stuffing.
- For juicier burgers, add 1/4 cup of wine, beer, ketchup, steak sauce, barbecue sauce, vegetable juice cocktail, canned onion soup or sour cream dip to each pound of ground beef.
- Don't stop with ordinary hot dogs—try different kinds such as smoked and cheese-flavored. Experiment with chubbies, bratwurst and smoked sausage.

Chip & Dip Burgers

Substitute your own favorite dip for Cheddar cheese sour cream dip.

8 oz. ground beef
1/4 cup crushed potato chips
1/4 cup Cheddar cheese sour cream dip
2 tablespoons pickle relish

2 hamburger rolls, warmed
1/4 cup Cheddar cheese sour cream dip
1/4 cup crushed potato chips

In a medium bowl, combine beef, 1/4 cup crushed potato chips, 1/4 cup sour cream dip and relish; mix well. Shape mixture into 2 patties. Cook patties in a medium skillet over medium heat about 15 minutes until done as desired, turning frequently. Serve on bottom halves of rolls. Top each burger with 2 tablespoons sour cream dip, 2 tablespoons crushed potato chips and top half of roll. Makes 2 servings.

Dilly Zucchini Burgers

Make tasty relish from your bumper zucchini crop.

3 tablespoons cider vinegar
1 tablespoon sugar
1 tablespoon water
1/4 teaspoon celery salt
1/4 cup thin zucchini slices
1 tablespoon chopped green onion

1 tablespoon dried parsley flakes
1/2 teaspoon dried dillweed
8 oz. ground beef
2 tablespoons chopped dill pickle
2 whole-wheat hamburger rolls, warmed

In a small bowl, combine vinegar, sugar, water and celery salt; mix well. Add zucchini, onion, parsley flakes and dillweed; toss to coat. Refrigerate 2 hours. Shape ground beef into 2 patties. Cook patties in a medium skillet over medium heat about 15 minutes until done as desired, turning frequently. Drain zucchini relish. Stir in chopped dill pickle. Serve burgers on bottom halves of rolls. Top each burger with zucchini relish mixture and top half of roll. Makes 2 servings.

Tostada Burgers

A bottle of sangria will go well with these open-face Mexican-style burgers.

1/2 cup refried beans
1 tablespoon taco seasoning mix
2 tostada shells
1 (8-oz.) can mixed vegetables, drained
2 tablespoons red wine salad dressing
1/2 teaspoon chili powder

8 oz. ground beef
Crisp lettuce leaves
2 slices tomato
Shredded process American cheese
Taco sauce
Pickled chili peppers

Mix refried beans and seasoning mix in a small bowl. Spread on tostada shells. In another small bowl, mix vegetables, salad dressing and chili powder. Spoon over beans on tostada shells. Shape beef into 2 patties. Cook patties in a medium skillet over medium heat about 15 minutes until done as desired, turning frequently. Place cooked patties on top of vegetables. Top each burger with lettuce, tomato and cheese. Serve with taco sauce and chili peppers. Makes 2 servings.

Slaw Burgers

Burgers cook best in a heavy skillet over medium or medium-high heat.

1/4 cup shredded cabbage
1 tablespoon shredded carrot
1 tablespoon chopped radish
1/4 teaspoon celery seeds

1/2 cup horseradish and bacon sour cream dip
8 oz. ground beef
2 slices rye toast

In a small bowl, mix cabbage, carrot, radish and celery seeds. Toss with 1/4 cup dip; chill. In a medium bowl, combine remaining dip and beef; mix well. Shape into 2 patties. Cook patties in a medium skillet over medium heat about 15 minutes until done as desired, turning frequently. Serve open-face on rye toast. Top each burger with chilled cole slaw. Makes 2 servings.

Tostada Burger

Mushroom Burgers Deluxe

Whip up these bacon-mushroom stuffed burgers for unexpected guests.

3 slices bacon
1/2 cup fresh mushroom slices
1/4 teaspoon garlic salt

12 oz. ground beef
2 hamburger rolls, warmed
Canned French-fried onions, warmed

Cook bacon in a large skillet until crisp. Drain; reserve drippings in skillet. Crumble bacon and set aside. Add mushrooms and garlic salt to drippings. Cook and stir until mushrooms are barely tender. Add mushrooms to bacon; reserve drippings in skillet. Shape beef into 4 thin patties. Spoon mushroom-bacon mixture onto centers of 2 patties. Cover with remaining patties; seal edges with your fingertips. Cook patties in skillet over medium-high heat about 8 minutes or until browned well on one side. Carefully turn patties. Reduce heat and cover patties loosely. Cook 6 to 7 minutes longer or until done as desired. Place on bottom halves of rolls. Top with French-fried onions and top halves of rolls. Makes 2 servings.

Burgundy Burgers

Try toasting the French bread in the skillet before cooking the burgers.

8 oz. ground beef
2 tablespoons Burgundy wine
Dash garlic salt
2 tablespoons butter or margarine

1/2 cup fresh mushroom slices
2 tablespoons chopped green onion
1/4 cup Burgundy wine
2 slices French bread

In a medium bowl, mix beef, 2 tablespoons Burgundy and garlic salt. Shape into 2 patties. Cook patties in a medium skillet over medium heat about 15 minutes until done as desired, turning frequently. Remove from skillet and keep warm. Melt butter or margarine in skillet. Add mushrooms and onion. Cook and stir until tender. Stir in remaining 1/4 cup Burgundy. Cook and stir until heated through. Serve patties on French bread. Top each burger with mushroom sauce. Makes 2 servings.

Health Burgers

Toast sunflower seeds in a 300°F (150°C) oven for 15 to 20 minutes, turning frequently.

4 oz. ground ham
4 oz. ground pork
2 tablespoons grated carrot
2 tablespoons raisins
1 tablespoon toasted sunflower seeds

2 tablespoons vegetable oil
2 whole-wheat hamburger rolls, warmed
Alfalfa sprouts
2 slices pineapple
Chutney

In a medium bowl, mix ham and pork. Shape into 4 thin patties. In a small bowl, mix carrot, raisins and sunflower seeds. Spoon onto centers of 2 patties. Cover with remaining patties; seal edges with your fingertips. Heat oil in a medium, heavy skillet. Cook patties in oil 6 to 7 minutes over medium-high heat until browned well on one side. Carefully turn patties. Reduce heat and cover. Cook until well-done, 7 to 8 minutes. Place patties on bottom halves of rolls. Top each burger with alfalfa sprouts, a pineapple slice, chutney and top half of roll. Makes 2 servings.

How to Make Health Burgers

1/Spoon carrot filling on half the pork burgers. Top with other burgers; seal edges with your fingertips.

2/Serve burgers on whole-wheat hamburger rolls. Top with alfalfa sprouts, a pineapple ring and chutney.

Guacamole Burgers

If you're in a hurry, substitute thawed frozen guacamole dip for the avocado mixture.

1 avocado, peeled, seeded, mashed
1 tablespoon canned chopped green chilies
1 teaspoon grated onion
1 tablespoon lemon juice
1/2 teaspoon garlic salt
8 oz. ground beef

1 small tomato, peeled, chopped
1/2 teaspoon garlic salt
1/2 teaspoon chili powder
2 slices French bread, toasted
Corn chips

In a small bowl, combine avocado, chilies, onion, lemon juice and 1/2 teaspoon garlic salt; mix well and chill. In a medium bowl, mix beef, tomato, 1/2 teaspoon garlic salt and chili powder. Shape into 2 patties. Cook patties in a medium skillet over medium heat about 15 minutes until done as desired, turning frequently. Serve on toasted French bread. Top burgers with chilled avocado mixture and corn chips. Makes 2 servings.

Greek Isle Burgers

Yogurt and mint add a Mediterranean touch to lamb burgers.

1/4 cup chopped, peeled cucumber
2 tablespoons chopped green onion
1/2 teaspoon dried leaf mint
1 teaspoon vegetable oil
12 oz. ground lamb
3 tablespoons plain yogurt
Garlic salt

Salt and pepper
2 Kaiser rolls, split
Crisp lettuce leaves
1 tomato, sliced
Crumbled feta cheese
Dried leaf oregano

In a small bowl, mix cucumber, green onion, mint and oil; set aside. In a medium bowl, mix lamb and yogurt. Shape into 4 very thin patties. Sprinkle with garlic salt. Spoon cucumber mixture onto centers of 2 patties. Cover with remaining patties. Seal edges with your fingertips. Cook patties in a medium skillet over medium heat 8 to 9 minutes or until browned well on one side. Carefully turn patties; season with salt and pepper. Reduce heat and cover loosely. Cook about 7 minutes longer or until done as desired. Place patties on bottom halves of Kaiser rolls. Place lettuce leaves, tomato slices and feta cheese on each pattie. Sprinkle with oregano. Top with top halves of rolls. Makes 2 servings.

Porcupine Burgers

Rice and beef topped with spicy tomato sauce make a complete meal.

8 oz. ground beef	Salt and pepper
1/4 cup cooked rice	1 tablespoon Worcestershire sauce
2 tablespoons chopped onion	1 teaspoon prepared mustard
1/2 (10-1/2-oz.) can condensed tomato soup	2 hamburger rolls, warmed
1/2 teaspoon dried leaf basil	Green pepper rings

In a medium bowl, combine beef, rice, onion, 2 tablespoons of the condensed soup and basil; mix well. Shape into 2 patties. Cook patties in a medium skillet over medium heat about 15 minutes until done as desired, turning frequently. Season with salt and pepper. In a small saucepan, combine remaining condensed soup, Worcestershire sauce and mustard. Cook and stir until heated through. Place patties on bottom halves of rolls. Spoon tomato sauce over patties. Garnish with green pepper rings. Top with top halves of rolls. Makes 2 servings.

Sausage-Stuffed Pork Burgers

Herb-seasoned stuffing and sausage lend a spicy flavor to this juicy burger.

3 oz. bulk pork sausage	8 oz. ground pork
1 tablespoon chopped onion	2 hamburger rolls, warmed
1 tablespoon chopped celery	Cranberry-orange relish
3 tablespoons herb-seasoned breadcrumbs for stuffing	

In a small skillet, cook sausage, onion and celery, stirring often, until meat is browned and vegetables are tender. Stir in breadcrumbs. Shape ground pork into 4 very thin patties. Spoon stuffing mixture onto centers of 2 patties. Cover with remaining patties. Seal edges with your fingertips. Cook patties in a large skillet over medium-high heat 6 to 7 minutes or until browned well on one side. Carefully turn patties. Reduce heat and cover loosely. Cook about 7 minutes longer or until well-done. Place on bottom halves of rolls. Top with cranberry-orange relish and top halves of rolls. Makes 2 servings.

Beer & Onion Burgers

Onions sautéed in beer garnish this juicy burger.

8 oz. ground beef
1/4 cup beer
1 teaspoon seasoned salt
2 Kaiser rolls, split
2 tablespoons butter or margarine
1 small onion, sliced, separated in rings

1/4 cup beer
1 tablespoon steak sauce
1/4 teaspoon dried leaf basil
1/4 teaspoon dried leaf thyme
Lettuce and tomato slices, if desired

In a medium bowl, mix beef, 1/4 cup beer and seasoned salt. Shape into 2 patties. Cook patties in a medium skillet over medium heat about 15 minutes until done as desired, turning frequently. Place on bottom halves of rolls and keep warm. Melt butter or margarine in skillet. Add onion. Cook and stir until tender. Stir in remaining 1/4 cup beer, steak sauce, basil and thyme. Cook and stir until heated through. Spoon onion mixture on top of patties. Top with top halves of rolls. Serve with lettuce and tomato slices, if desired. Makes 2 servings.

Curry Condiment Burgers

Chutney makes an unusual topping for an exotic burger.

2 tablespoons chopped salted peanuts
1 tablespoon flaked coconut
1 tablespoon raisins
12 oz. ground beef

1/2 teaspoon curry powder
Salt and pepper
2 hamburger rolls, warmed
Chutney

In a small bowl, mix peanuts, coconut and raisins; set aside. In a medium bowl, combine beef and curry powder; mix well. Shape into 4 very thin patties. Spoon peanut mixture onto centers of 2 patties. Cover with remaining patties; seal edges with your fingertips. Cook patties in a large skillet over medium-high heat about 8 minutes or until browned well on one side. Carefully turn patties. Season with salt and pepper. Reduce heat and cover loosely. Cook 6 to 7 minutes longer or until done as desired. Place on bottom halves of rolls. Top with chutney and top halves of rolls. Makes 2 servings.

Beer & Onion Burger

Sausage & Egg Sandwich

Try this one for breakfast, lunch or dinner.

2 tablespoons butter or margarine, softened
2 teaspoons prepared mustard
2 slices bread, toasted
1 (5- to 6-oz.) large fully cooked
  smoked link sausage, halved

1 tablespoon vegetable oil
2 eggs
2 slices American cheese
Relish or green pepper, if desired

Combine butter or margarine and mustard in a small bowl. Beat to blend well. Spread on toast slices. Split sausage halves lengthwise, cutting to other side but not through. Open and place in a medium skillet. Cook until heated through, 3 to 5 minutes on each side. Place sausage on toast slices and keep warm. Add oil to skillet. Cook eggs in oil until set. Turn and cook until done as desired. Place each egg on top of a sausage half. Top with cheese slices. Serve with relish or green pepper, if desired. Makes 2 servings.

Cheese-Topped Garden Burgers

Double-cheese topping makes outstanding burgers.

1/4 cup shredded sharp Cheddar cheese
2 tablespoons creamy blue cheese
  salad dressing
2 tablespoons dairy sour cream
8 oz. ground beef
2 tablespoons quick-cooking oats
1/2 teaspoon instant minced onion

1 tablespoon creamy blue cheese
  salad dressing
1/4 teaspoon celery salt
1 tablespoon butter or margarine, softened
2 slices French bread
Crisp lettuce leaves
4 tomato slices

In a small bowl, combine Cheddar cheese, 2 tablespoons salad dressing and sour cream; set aside. In a medium bowl, thoroughly combine ground beef, oats, instant minced onion, 1 tablespoon salad dressing and celery salt; mix well. Preheat broiler. Shape meat mixture into 2 oval patties. Place on rack on unheated broiler pan. Broil at medium temperature about 5 inches from the heat 4 to 5 minutes. Turn and broil 4 to 5 minutes longer or until done as desired. Spread butter or margarine on French bread slices. Place bread on broiler pan with patties during the last few minutes of cooking time. Place lettuce, then patties on toasted bread. Place tomato slices on top of each burger. Top with Cheddar cheese mixture. Makes 2 servings.

Pizza Burger Dogs

It's easier to mold ground beef around frankfurters when it's chilled.

1 egg
1 slice bread, torn in bite-size pieces
1/2 teaspoon chili powder
1/4 teaspoon salt
1/4 teaspoon dried leaf oregano
1/4 teaspoon ground cumin

8 oz. ground beef
3 frankfurters
2 tablespoons vegetable oil
3 hot dog rolls, warmed
Canned pizza sauce, warmed
Grated Parmesan cheese

In a medium bowl, beat together egg and bread. Stir in chili powder, salt, oregano and cumin. Add beef; mix thoroughly. Divide into 3 portions. Wrap each portion in waxed paper; chill. Shape each chilled portion around a frankfurter, covering completely. Add oil to large skillet. Cook burger dogs over medium heat about 12 minutes, turning several times to cook all sides. Cover loosely during last 5 minutes of cooking time. Place on hot dog rolls. Spoon pizza sauce over burger dogs. Sprinkle with Parmesan cheese. Makes 3 servings.

How to Make Pizza Burger Dogs

Divide ground beef mixture into 3 equal portions. Shape each portion into a long oval patty. Mold patty around hot dog.

Jiffy Hot Dog Suppers

- Sauté frankfurter chunks, chopped onion and chopped green pepper in a little butter or margarine. Stir in bottled barbecue sauce and heat through. Serve over hot cooked rice.

- Broil or grill frankfurters. Place each frankfurter on a warm tortilla. Top with shredded Monterey Jack cheese and chopped canned green chilies. Roll up and serve immediately.

- Place grilled frankfurters in buns. Top with hot canned chili. Sprinkle with grated sharp Cheddar cheese and chopped green onions. Serve at once.

Frankly Hot Three-Bean Salad

Use jumbo frankfurters for man-size appetites.

3 slices bacon
1/4 cup chopped onion
1 (8-oz.) can kidney beans, drained
1 (8-oz.) can wax beans, drained

1 (8-oz.) can green beans, drained
1/4 cup French dressing with spices and herbs
2 tablespoons chopped pimiento
4 large frankfurters

Cook bacon in a medium skillet until crisp. Drain; reserve drippings in skillet. Crumble bacon and set aside. Add onion to bacon drippings. Cook and stir until tender. Stir in kidney beans, wax beans, green beans, French dressing and pimiento. Cook until heated through, stirring gently. Remove bean salad from skillet; keep warm. Deeply score frankfurters diagonally at 1/2-inch intervals. Place in a bowl of hot water. Let stand 30 seconds. Remove frankfurters from water and place in skillet. Cook and turn over medium-high heat until frankfurters are curled and heated through, 4 to 5 minutes. Spoon hot bean salad inside curve of frankfurters. Top with crumbled bacon. Makes 4 servings.

Italian Sausage Sandwich

This hearty sandwich is a favorite at Italian street fairs.

2 tablespoons vegetable oil
1 (8-oz.) fully cooked Italian sausage
   link, cut in 1-inch pieces
1/4 cup chopped onion
1/4 cup chopped green pepper

1 garlic clove, minced
1-1/4 cups bottled Italian cooking sauce
2 teaspoons sugar
1 teaspoon chili powder
2 submarine rolls or French rolls, split

Heat oil in a medium skillet. Add sausage, onion, green pepper and garlic. Stir over medium heat until sausage is browned. Add Italian cooking sauce, sugar and chili powder. Stir until heated through. Place on bottom halves of rolls. Top with top halves of rolls. Makes 2 servings.

Bratwurst & Sauerkraut

Be sure the bratwurst you use is labeled fully cooked.

3 fully cooked bratwurst (6-oz.),
  cut in 1-inch pieces
1 (8-oz.) can sauerkraut, drained, rinsed

1/2 cup chopped green onion
1 teaspoon caraway seeds
2 onion rolls, split, warmed

In a medium skillet, cook bratwurst over medium-high heat 8 to 9 minutes or until browned well on all sides. Reduce heat to medium-low. Stir in sauerkraut, onion and caraway seeds. Stir until heated through. Serve on bottom halves of rolls. Top with top halves of rolls. Makes 2 servings.

Tangy Barbecued Franks

Barbecue sauce tastes best when you make it yourself.

Vegetable oil
4 frankfurters
1 (8-oz.) can tomato sauce
1/4 cup packed brown sugar

1 tablespoon Worcestershire sauce
1 tablespoon prepared mustard
1/4 teaspoon hot pepper sauce
4 hot dog rolls, warmed

Brush a medium skillet with oil. Add frankfurters and cook over medium-high heat until browned on all sides. Reduce heat to medium-low. In a small bowl, mix tomato sauce, brown sugar, Worcestershire sauce, mustard and hot pepper sauce. Pour sauce over frankfurters. Cook and stir until sauce is heated through. Serve on hot dog rolls. Makes 4 servings.

Sloppy Joes

Yummy Joes would be a better name!

8 oz. ground beef
2 tablespoons chopped onion
2 tablespoons chopped green pepper
2 tablespoons chopped celery
1/4 teaspoon garlic salt

1/2 cup ketchup
1 teaspoon prepared mustard
1 teaspoon Worcestershire sauce
3 hamburger rolls, warmed

In a medium skillet, combine beef, onion, green pepper, celery and garlic salt. Cook and stir until meat is browned and vegetables are tender. Drain off excess fat. Stir in ketchup, mustard and Worcestershire sauce. Cook and stir until heated through. Spoon mixture onto bottom halves of rolls. Top with top halves of rolls. Makes 3 servings.

Idaho Favorite

Try this out on your meat-and-potato enthusiasts!

2/3 cup instant mashed potato flakes
1/2 cup shredded Cheddar cheese
1/4 cup dairy sour cream
2 tablespoons dried chives

1 cup boiling water
6 frankfurters
1 tablespoon vegetable oil
6 hot dog rolls, warmed

In a small bowl, mix potato flakes, cheese, sour cream and chives. Pour boiling water over potato mixture; mix well. Cut lengthwise slits in frankfurters, cutting to other side but not through. Fill slits with potato mixture. Heat oil in a large skillet. Cook frankfurters in oil over medium heat until heated through, turning to cook all sides. Serve on hot dog rolls. Makes 6 servings.

Inside-Out Corn Dogs

Enjoy satisfying corn dog flavor without deep-frying.

4 oz. bulk pork sausage
1 tablespoon chopped celery
1 tablespoon chopped onion
1 cup corn bread stuffing mix
1/4 cup water
4 jumbo frankfurters

1 tablespoon butter or margarine
2 tablespoons chopped onion
2 tablespoons canned chopped green chilies
1 garlic clove, minced
1 (8-oz.) can tomatoes, drained, mashed
4 hot dog rolls, warmed

In a large skillet, cook sausage, celery and 1 tablespoon onion until sausage is browned and vegetables are tender. Place in a large bowl; reserve drippings in skillet. Add stuffing mix and water to sausage mixture; mix well. Cut lengthwise slits in frankfurters, cutting to other side but not through. Fill slits with stuffing mixture. Cook stuffed frankfurters in sausage drippings until heated through, turning often. Melt butter or margarine in a small saucepan. Add 2 tablespoons chopped onion, green chilies and garlic. Cook until onion is tender. Add tomatoes; heat through. Serve frankfurters on hot dog rolls with tomato sauce. Makes 4 servings.

Polynesian Stuffed Bratwurst

Delicious as hors d'oeuvres, too. Cut them in pieces and serve them with cocktail picks.

4 smoked fully cooked bratwurst
   (about 12 oz.)
2 tablespoons prepared mustard

1 (8-oz.) can pineapple chunks, drained
4 slices bacon
4 hot dog rolls, warmed

Cut lengthwise slits in bratwurst, cutting to other side but not through. Spread inside of slits with mustard. Cut pineapple chunks in half and place in slits. Wrap bacon around bratwurst, securing with wooden picks. Cook in a large skillet over medium-high heat. Turn often until bacon is done and bratwurst is heated through, 8 to 10 minutes. Serve on hot dog rolls. Makes 4 servings.

How to Make Polynesian Stuffed Bratwurst

1/Split bratwurst lengthwise, cutting to but not through other side. Spread inside of slit with mustard. Stuff the slits with pineapple chunks.

2/Wind bacon around each bratwurst. Insert wooden picks diagonally to secure bacon. Toothpicks inserted crosswise make poor use of skillet space.

Fast Sandwich Suppers

Sandwiches served with a mug of soup or seasoned broth are fast and filling. Dessert can be sliced fresh fruit or canned mixed fruit. A sandwich doesn't have to be 5 inches high with thick slabs of bread at each end. Do as the Scandinavians do: Layer the fillings on one piece of bread for an open-face sandwich.

With a sandwich supper in mind, you can stop by the deli and take home all the makings of a sandwich buffet. A deli offers an assortment of cold cuts and other sliced cooked meats, a variety of cheeses—some you've probably never tasted—and a selection of breads and rolls. Don't forget to investigate the salad trays where you're likely to discover potato salad, cole slaw, macaroni salad, pickled vegetables and stuffed eggs. While your purchases are being weighed and wrapped, wander through the shelf displays to see what else is available. You'll find soup mixes and canned chowders, exotic fruit juices, canned fish, sandwich spreads and imported cookies to match up with fruit for dessert.

If you shy away from sandwiches because they always seem to be laden with calories, here's a dieter's delight: Mix some shredded cheese with a little skim milk, dry mustard and a dash of Worcestershire sauce. Spread the mixture on thin slices of whole-wheat toast. Broil until the cheese mixture is bubbly and serve immediately.

How about a sandwich without bread? Let high-protein, low-calorie meat slices take the place of bread.

● Spread a slice of turkey with horseradish mustard. Then place a green pepper ring, fresh mushroom slices, bean sprouts or alfafa sprouts, chopped water chestnuts and a slice of tomato on the turkey. Drizzle with diet dressing and serve immediately with a knife and fork.

● Spread thinly sliced ham with mustard. Add a spoonful of potato salad and shredded Cheddar cheese. Roll up and serve with a knife and fork or on a hot dog bun with sweet pickle relish.

● Spread horseradish sauce on a thin slice of roast beef. Top with a spoonful of cole slaw and chopped tomato. Roll up. Serve with a knife and fork or on a hot dog bun with mustard relish.

● Spread a slice of corned beef with Dijon-style mustard. Add some sauerkraut salad, shredded Swiss cheese and dill pickle chips. Roll up and serve with a knife and fork or on a crusty rye roll.

Steak & Cheese Subs

Thinly sliced sirloin tip is often labeled breakfast steak *and is usually an economical buy.*

3 tablespoons butter or margarine	**2 slices Cheddar cheese**
1 onion, sliced, separated in rings	**2 submarine rolls or French rolls, split**
2 (3-oz.) thinly sliced sirloin tip steaks	**Crisp lettuce leaves**
Garlic salt	**4 or more slices tomato**
Pepper	**Horseradish sauce**

Melt butter or margarine in a large skillet. Cook and stir onion in butter or margarine over medium-high heat until tender. Remove from skillet and keep warm. Sprinkle sirloin tip slices with garlic salt and pepper. Cook in skillet over medium-high heat until browned. Turn and top with cheese slices. Cook until done as desired. Place on bottom halves of rolls. Top with grilled onions, lettuce leaves and tomato slices. Spread with horseradish sauce. Top with top halves of rolls. Makes 2 servings.

Hearty Roast Beef Sandwiches

Sunday's pot roast tastes even better on Monday with this creamy sauce.

Creamy Mustard Sauce, see below	**1 tablespoon all-purpose flour**
2 tablespoons butter or margarine	**1/2 cup beef broth**
2 slices cooked roast beef	**1 teaspoon Worcestershire sauce**
2 slices white bread, lightly toasted	**Salt and pepper**
1 tablespoon butter or margarine	

Creamy Mustard Sauce:
2 tablespoons dairy sour cream
1 teaspoon Dijon-style mustard

Prepare Creamy Mustard Sauce; set aside. Melt 2 tablespoons butter or margarine in a medium skillet. Cook and turn roast beef in butter or margarine until heated through. Place on toast and keep warm. Melt 1 tablespoon butter or margarine in skillet. Stir in flour. Add beef broth and Worcestershire sauce. Cook and stir over medium-high heat until thickened and bubbly. Season to taste with salt and pepper. Spoon over roast beef and toast. Top with a dollop of Creamy Mustard Sauce. Makes 2 servings.

Creamy Mustard Sauce:
Mix sour cream and mustard in a small bowl. Makes about 2-1/2 tablespoons of sauce.

Crunchy Ham Sandwiches

Crunchy outside with a complete meal inside!

4 slices white bread
1 tablespoon butter or margarine, softened
1 tablespoon prepared mustard
2 slices cooked ham
2 slices process American cheese
4 thin slices tomato

1 egg, slightly beaten
1 tablespoon milk
Dash onion salt
3/4 cup crushed corn chips or potato chips
2 tablespoons vegetable oil

Spread 2 bread slices on 1 side with butter or margarine. Spread remaining 2 bread slices on 1 side with mustard. Top each mustard-spread slice with 1 slice ham, 1 slice cheese and 2 slices tomato. Place a slice of bread buttered-side down on top of tomato. In a pie plate, mix egg, milk and onion salt. Dip sandwiches in egg mixture, then in crushed corn chips or potato chips. Pat to secure chips to bread, turning to coat both sides. Add oil to preheated griddle or skillet. Cook sandwiches in oil until golden brown on one side. Turn and cook until golden brown on second side. Makes 2 servings.

How to Make Crunchy Ham Sandwiches

Spread bread with mustard, then add ham, cheese and tomato slices. Cover with another bread slice. Dip sandwich in egg mixture before grilling.

Quick Grilled Sandwiches

- For a delicious golden-grilled supper, dip almost any sandwich in a mixture of 1 egg, 1 tablespoon of milk and a dash of flavored salt, then coat with crushed chips or crackers. Cook on both sides in a hot oiled skillet until golden brown.

- Spread rye bread with Thousand Island Dressing. Layer with different kinds of salami, deli potato salad and Swiss cheese. Cover with a bread slice. Dip in the egg mixture and crushed sesame crackers, then grill.

- Spread bread with mustard. Layer with roast beef, deli cole slaw and dill pickle slices. Top with a bread slice. Dip in the egg mixture and crushed potato chips before grilling.

- Layer bread with deli chicken salad, cranberry-orange relish and chopped nuts. Top with a bread slice. Dip in the egg mixture and then in herb-seasoned stuffing before grilling.

Athenian-Style Lamb & Pita

If all the ingredients aren't in your supermarket, check local delicatessens and specialty stores.

Cucumber-Garlic Sauce, see below
1 tablespoon vegetable oil
12 oz. lamb, cut in 1/2-inch cubes
2 tablespoons chopped onion
2 tablespoons chopped green pepper
1/2 teaspoon dried leaf oregano, crushed

1/2 teaspoon garlic salt
2 to 4 pita breads, halved crosswise
Chopped tomato
Ripe olive slices
Crumbled feta cheese
Additional oregano, if desired

Cucumber-Garlic Sauce:
1 cup plain yogurt
1 medium cucumber, grated

1/2 teaspoon garlic salt

Prepare Cucumber-Garlic Sauce; set aside. Heat oil in a medium skillet. Add lamb cubes, onion, green pepper, oregano and garlic salt to oil. Cook and stir over medium-high heat until lamb is done as desired. Spoon lamb mixture into pita bread halves. Top with tomato, olives, cheese, Cucumber-Garlic Sauce and additional oregano, if desired. Makes 2 to 4 servings.

Cucumber-Garlic Sauce:
In a small bowl, mix yogurt, cucumber and garlic salt. Makes 1-1/2 cups of sauce.

Deluxe BLTs

Horseradish sauce resembles salad dressing or mayonnaise flavored with horseradish.

4 slices white bread, lightly toasted
2 slices sharp Cheddar cheese
2 tablespoons horseradish sauce

Crisp lettuce leaves
4 slices bacon, cooked crisp, drained
1 tomato, sliced

Top 2 toast slices with cheese. Spread remaining 2 toast slices with horseradish sauce and top with lettuce leaves. Top with bacon and tomato slices. Cover with remaining toast slices, cheese-side down. Makes 2 servings.

Athenian-Style Lamb & Pita

Neptune's Delight

A great catch in taste, economy and nutrition!

2 tablespoons vegetable oil
1 (8-oz.) pkg. frozen fried breaded
 fish fillets
3 sesame seed hamburger rolls, warmed
1/4 cup mayonnaise

2 tablespoons chopped dill pickle
1 tablespoon chopped green olives
1 tablespoon lemon juice
1 hard-cooked egg, sliced

Heat oil in a preheated large skillet. Cook fish in oil until browned on both sides and fish flakes easily with a fork. Place fish on bottom halves of rolls. In a small bowl, mix mayonnaise, pickle, olives and lemon juice. Spoon mayonnaise mixture on top of fish. Arrange egg slices on mayonnaise mixture. Top with top halves of rolls. Makes 3 servings.

Italian Meatball Submarines

Italian cooking sauce is similar to marinara sauce.

8 oz. bulk pork sausage
2 submarine rolls or French rolls, split
1/4 cup chopped onion

1/4 cup chopped green pepper
3/4 cup bottled Italian cooking sauce
1/2 cup shredded mozzarella cheese

Shape sausage into 1-inch balls. Cook sausage balls in a medium skillet over medium-high heat until browned well, turning often. Place on bottom halves of rolls and keep warm; reserve sausage drippings in skillet. Cook and stir onion and green pepper in sausage drippings until tender. Drain drippings. Add Italian cooking sauce to onion and green pepper in skillet. Cook and stir until heated through. Spoon sauce over meatballs. Sprinkle with mozzarella cheese. Top with top halves of rolls. Makes 2 servings.

Confetti Smoked Beef

An appetizing hot sandwich for a cold winter day. Serve it with a green salad.

2 slices white bread, toasted
1 tablespoon butter or margarine, softened
1 (3-oz.) pkg. sliced smoked beef
2 tablespoons butter or margarine
2 tablespoons all-purpose flour

1 cup milk
2 tablespoons chopped pimiento
2 teaspoons dried parsley flakes
Dash pepper

Spread toast with 1 tablespoon butter or margarine; keep warm. Tear beef into bite-size pieces. Melt 2 tablespoons butter or margarine in a medium skillet. Cook and turn beef in butter or margarine until heated through, about 2 minutes. Stir in flour. Add milk, pimiento, parsley flakes and pepper. Cook and stir over medium-high heat until thickened and bubbly. Serve over buttered toast. Makes 2 servings.

Hot Turkey Royale

A superb way to use leftover turkey.

1 (8-1/4-oz.) can asparagus spears, undrained	1 tablespoon all-purpose flour
	1/2 cup chicken broth
2 tablespoons butter or margarine	1 tablespoon dry white wine
2 slices cooked turkey	Salt and pepper
2 slices whole-wheat bread, toasted	2 tablespoons crumbled blue cheese

Heat asparagus in liquid in a small saucepan. Melt butter or margarine in a medium skillet. Cook and turn turkey in butter or margarine until heated through. Drain asparagus. Spoon hot asparagus on top of turkey. Place turkey and asparagus on toasted bread slices. Stir flour into juices in skillet. Add chicken broth and wine; stir well. Cook and stir over medium-high heat until mixture thickens and bubbles. Season with salt and pepper. Spoon sauce over turkey and asparagus. Sprinkle with blue cheese. Makes 2 servings.

Hot Tuna Sandwiches

Grapes and pineapple slices move tuna up on the gourmet scale.

1 tablespoon vegetable oil	1 hard-cooked egg, chopped
1/2 cup seedless green grapes	Crisp lettuce leaves
2 tablespoons chopped onion	6 slices white bread, toasted
2 tablespoons chopped celery	3 slices pineapple
1/4 cup Thousand Island dressing	Celery salt
1 (6-1/2-oz.) can tuna, drained	

Heat oil in a medium skillet. Cook grapes, onion and celery in oil over medium heat until onions are tender. Add dressing to skillet. Add tuna and egg to skillet. Stir gently until heated through. Place lettuce leaves on 3 bread slices. Top with tuna mixture and pineapple slices. Sprinkle with celery salt. Cover with remaining bread slices. Makes 3 servings.

Hot Club Sandwiches

Sunday's roast chicken becomes an easy supper later in the week.

3 slices bacon
2 English muffins, split
1 cup cubed cooked chicken
2 tablespoons chopped celery
2 tablespoons chopped pimiento

Salt and pepper
1/2 cup plain yogurt
2 tablespoons mayonnaise
2 slices tomato
1 avocado, peeled, seeded, sliced

Cook bacon in a large skillet until crisp. Drain; reserve 3 tablespoons drippings in a small bowl. Crumble bacon and set aside. Pour 2 tablespoons bacon drippings into skillet. Toast muffin halves cut-side down in drippings. Place on serving plates. Add remaining 1 tablespoon bacon drippings to skillet. Cook and stir chicken, celery and pimiento in drippings until heated through. Season with salt and pepper. Mix yogurt and mayonnaise in a small bowl. Spoon half the yogurt mixture into chicken mixture. Cook and stir until heated through. Spoon chicken mixture onto bottom halves of muffins. Place top halves of muffins on chicken mixture. Top with tomato and avocado slices. Spoon a dollop of remaining yogurt mixture on each sandwich. Sprinkle with crumbled bacon. Makes 2 servings.

Swiss Tenderloin Sandwiches

Delightful texture with a choice blending of flavors.

1 egg
1 tablespoon water
1 cup sesame-cheese cracker crumbs
2 pork tenderloins, flattened into rounds
1 tablespoon vegetable oil

1 slice Swiss cheese, halved diagonally
2 onion rolls, split, warmed
2 crisp lettuce leaves
2 tomato slices
Thousand Island dressing

In a pie plate, beat egg and water with a fork. Place cracker crumbs in another pie plate. Dip tenderloins in crumbs, then in egg, then again in crumbs. Add oil to preheated griddle. Cook tenderloins until browned on one side. Turn and place cheese triangles on tenderloins. Cook until other side is browned and tenderloins are no longer pink when cut. Place on bottom halves of rolls. Top with lettuce, tomato, Thousand Island dressing and top halves of rolls. Makes 2 servings.

Hot Club Sandwich

Shrimp Cocktail in a Bun

For an appetizer, serve shrimp pieces on wooden picks with a bowl of Cocktail Sauce.

1/4 cup vegetable oil
1 (9-oz.) pkg. frozen breaded shrimp sticks
3 hamburger rolls, warmed

Boston lettuce leaves
Cocktail Sauce, see below

Cocktail Sauce:
1/4 cup chili sauce
1 tablespoon prepared horseradish
1 tablespoon chopped onion

1 teaspoon lemon juice
1/2 teaspoon Worcestershire sauce

Heat oil in a medium skillet. Cook shrimp sticks in hot oil over medium-high heat until browned and shrimp flakes easily with a fork, turning several times. Serve on bottom halves of rolls with lettuce leaves and Cocktail Sauce. Top with top halves of rolls. Makes 3 servings.

Cocktail Sauce:
In a small saucepan, combine chili sauce, horseradish, onion, lemon juice and Worcestershire sauce. Cook and stir until heated through. Makes 1/3 cup of sauce.

How to Make Shrimp Cocktail in a Bun

Line bottoms of rolls with lettuce. Place crisp shrimp sticks on lettuce. Top with hot Cocktail Sauce.

Easy Frozen Fish Ideas

- Use Cocktail Sauce from Shrimp Cocktail in a Bun to top other fried breaded fish.
- Fry frozen breaded shrimp. Add hot bottled sweet-sour sauce, pineapple chunks and green pepper chunks. Serve on hot cooked rice.
- Serve fish and chips in the true English tradition. Fry or bake frozen breaded fish portions and frozen dinner fries. Serve on pieces of newspaper lined with waxed paper and pass plenty of white vinegar and salt.
- Cook and drain frozen chopped spinach. Mix spinach with tartar sauce and spread on a plate. Fry breaded scallops and serve on the spinach mixture.

Bagels with Creamy Salmon Filling

Smoked salmon is also known as lox.

2 tablespoons butter or margarine
2 bagels, split
2 oz. smoked salmon, flaked

1 (3-oz.) pkg. cream cheese, softened
2 tablespoons chopped pimiento

Melt butter or margarine in a large skillet. Toast bagels in skillet. Remove toasted bagels and keep warm. Cook and stir salmon in butter or margarine in skillet until heated through. Add more butter or margarine if needed. Remove from heat and mix in cream cheese and pimiento. Spread mixture on bottom halves of bagels. Top with top halves of bagels. Makes 2 servings.

Vegetarian Delight

A delicious nutrition-packed sandwich with freshness and crunch.

3 tablespoons butter or margarine
2 sesame seed hamburger rolls, split
2 slices Muenster cheese
2 slices sharp Cheddar cheese
1/4 cup chopped onion
1/2 medium carrot, grated

1/4 cup Italian salad dressing
Celery salt
6 slices cucumber
4 slices tomato
1/4 cup alfalfa sprouts

Melt butter or margarine in a medium skillet. Place top halves of hamburger rolls split-side down in skillet. Cook until toasted. Remove and top with Muenster cheese slices. Toast bottom halves of hamburger rolls split-side down. Remove from skillet and top with Cheddar cheese slices. Cook and stir onion, carrot, salad dressing and celery salt in skillet until vegetables are crisp-tender. Layer cucumber slices and tomato slices on bottom halves of rolls. Spoon onion-carrot mixture on top of tomato. Top with alfalfa sprouts and top halves of rolls. Makes 2 servings.

Grilled Guacamole Sandwiches

Enjoy the rich nutlike flavor of avocados!

1 avocado, peeled, seeded, mashed	**4 slices cracked-wheat bread**
2 tablespoons chopped onion	**1 tablespoon butter or margarine, softened**
2 tablespoons canned chopped green chilies	**4 thin slices tomato**
2 tablespoons mayonnaise	**2 slices Monterey Jack cheese**
1 teaspoon lemon juice	**1 tablespoon butter or margarine**

In a medium bowl, mix avocado, onion, chilies, mayonnaise and lemon juice. Spread on 2 bread slices. Spread remaining bread slices with 1 tablespoon butter or margarine. Top avocado filling with tomato and cheese. Cover with buttered bread slices buttered-side up. Melt 1 tablespoon butter or margarine on preheated griddle. Cook sandwiches buttered-side up in butter or margarine until golden brown on one side. Turn and brown on second side. Makes 2 servings.

Barbecue Pork Sandwiches

Turn leftover pork roast into a delicious hot sandwich.

1/2 cup ketchup	**Dash garlic powder**
2 tablespoons water	**Dash hot pepper sauce**
1 tablespoon Worcestershire sauce	**2 large slices cooked pork roast**
2 teaspoons brown sugar	**2 hamburger rolls, warmed**

In a medium skillet, mix ketchup, water, Worcestershire sauce, brown sugar, garlic powder and hot pepper sauce. Bring to a boil. Add pork. Reduce heat and simmer until pork is heated through, turning pork and spooning sauce over several times. Spoon pork and sauce onto bottom halves of rolls. Top with top halves of rolls. Makes 2 servings.

Grilled Cheese & Bacon Sandwiches

A hearty sandwich that's long on flavor.

1/2 cup shredded process American cheese	**2 tablespoons bacon bits**
2 tablespoons mayonnaise	**4 white bread slices**
2 tablespoons chopped pimiento	**Butter or margarine, softened**

In a small bowl, mix cheese, mayonnaise, pimiento and bacon bits. Spread 1 side of each bread slice with butter or margarine. Spread unbuttered side of 2 bread slices with cheese mixture. Top with remaining bread slices buttered-side up. Place sandwiches on preheated griddle. Cook until golden brown on one side. Turn and cook until other side is golden brown. Makes 2 servings.

Late Suppers

After the theater, sports event or bridge, invite a few friends over for a midnight repast. Omelets and pancakes are perfect for a small late crowd.

Most of the pancake recipes in this book call for pancake mix and give directions for adding eggs, oil and milk. However, your pancake mix may be *complete* which means it already contains eggs, oil and milk. You may use complete pancake mix in these recipes if you first prepare the pancake batter according to the package directions, then follow my instructions for adding the other ingredients. For instance, if the recipe calls for 2 cups of pancake mix plus an egg, oil and milk, use 2 cups of complete pancake mix with the amount of liquid suggested on the package for making the pancake batter, then continue with the recipe.

Tender golden pancakes are irresistible. For best results, use a whisk to mix the pancake batter. Beat just until the batter is fairly smooth with some lumps. Do not overbeat. Preheat your griddle. When a few drops of water sprinkled on the griddle sizzle, the griddle is ready. As the underside of the pancake bakes, bubbles will form on the top of the pancake. When the bubbles burst, the pancake is ready to be turned.

You don't have to limit late suppers to omelets and pancakes. You probably have the makings for a superb midnight supper in your refrigerator right now.

● Raid-the-refrigerator tacos are always a treat. Fill a colorful serving bowl with chopped leftover meat, browned ground beef, salami strips or chopped canned meat. Set out a basket of crisp packaged taco shells. Spoon the meat into the taco shells and top it with shredded lettuce, chopped tomato, shredded cheese, canned chopped green chilies and taco sauce.

● Fill frozen crepes with frozen spinach soufflé, frozen chicken a la king or frozen broccoli with cheese sauce. Bake until the sauce is bubbly.

● Pop frozen waffles in the toaster. Top them with fresh or canned fruit, ice cream sauce and scoops of ice cream or whipped topping. Put everything on the table and let your guests make their own.

● For homemade pizza, start with plain refrigerated pizza crust. Layer it with tomato paste, pepperoni, olives, fennel seeds, oregano, chopped green pepper and shredded mozzarella cheese. Or cut the plain crust in wedges so your guests can layer pizza toppings according to their own tastes. If you don't have a pizza crust, use English muffins.

● Cut pita bread in half and fill the pockets with nut butters, fresh fruit, shredded cheese and then drizzle the filling with honey.

● Set up a burger bar. Broil, grill or fry burgers—better yet, let your guests cook their own. Serve the burgers on thick slices of toasted French bread. Bacon bits, sautéed mushrooms, canned French fried onions and frozen Welsh rarebit will add the finishing touches.

● Ladle steaming soup into thick mugs—use canned soup improved with seasonings, wine or vegetables, or combine one canned soup with another. Arrange a variety of crackers on a broiler-proof platter. Top them with cheese and broil briefly to melt the cheese. A fast relish tray of canned spiced peaches, olives, pickles and marinated artichokes will round out this appetizing snack-supper.

Sausage & Sour Cream Omelet

This rich omelet is one of my favorites.

8 oz. bulk pork sausage
2 tablespoons chopped green onion
1/2 cup dairy sour cream
4 eggs

2 tablespoons water
1/2 teaspoon celery salt
2 tablespoons vegetable oil

In a small skillet, cook and stir sausage and onion until sausage is browned. Remove from heat; drain off drippings. Stir sour cream into sausage. Keep warm but do not boil. In a small bowl, combine eggs, water and celery salt. Beat with a fork or whisk until mixed well but not frothy. In an 8-inch omelet pan or skillet, heat 1 tablespoon oil over medium-high heat. When a drop of water sizzles in the pan, pour in half the egg mixture. Cook, gently lifting edges so uncooked portion flows underneath, until eggs are set. Spoon half the sausage filling onto omelet; roll up. Remove from pan. Repeat with remaining oil, egg mixture and filling. Makes 2 servings.

Sausage Roll-Up

This protein-packed omelet will keep you going all through a busy morning.

2 pork sausage links
2 eggs
1 tablespoon milk
1/8 teaspoon salt

Dash pepper
1 tablespoon vegetable oil
1 slice process American cheese

Cook sausage links as directed on package. Remove from heat and keep warm. In a small bowl, combine eggs, milk, salt and pepper. Beat with a fork or whisk until mixed well but not frothy. In an 8-inch omelet pan or skillet, heat oil over medium-high heat. When a drop of water sizzles in the pan, pour in egg mixture. Cook, gently lifting edges so uncooked portion flows underneath, until eggs are set. Place cheese and sausage on top of omelet; roll up. Makes 1 serving.

Creamy Tomato Omelet

Cottage cheese and tomato make a wonderful creamy filling.

1 tablespoon vegetable oil
1/4 cup chopped tomato
1/4 cup cottage cheese with chives
2 eggs

1 tablespoon milk
1/8 teaspoon salt
Dash pepper
1 tablespoon vegetable oil

Heat 1 tablespoon oil in a small skillet. Add tomato. Cook and stir until heated through. Remove from heat and stir in cottage cheese; set aside. In a small bowl, combine eggs, milk, salt and pepper. Beat with a fork or whisk until mixed well but not frothy. In an 8-inch omelet pan or skillet, heat 1 tablespoon oil over medium-high heat. When a drop of water sizzles in the pan, pour in egg mixture. Cook, gently lifting edges so uncooked portion flows underneath, until eggs are set. Spoon cottage cheese and tomato onto omelet; roll up. Makes 1 serving.

Omelet Divan

Easy cheese sauce with broccoli rounds out an appealing and nutritious omelet.

1 (10-oz.) pkg. frozen broccoli in
  cheese sauce, thawed
4 eggs
2 tablespoons milk

1/2 teaspoon celery salt
Dash pepper
2 tablespoons vegetable oil

Cook broccoli in cheese sauce according to package directions. Remove from heat; keep warm. In small bowl, combine eggs, milk, celery salt and pepper. Beat with a fork or whisk until mixed well but not frothy. In an 8-inch omelet pan or skillet, heat 1 tablespoon oil over medium-high heat. When a drop of water sizzles in the pan, pour in half the egg mixture. Cook, gently lifting edges so uncooked portion flows underneath, until eggs are set. Spoon half the broccoli filling onto omelet; roll up. Remove from pan. Add remaining oil to pan. Repeat with remaining egg mixture and broccoli filling. Makes 2 servings.

Mexicali Omelet

Avocado dip and hot pepper sauce bring Mexican sunshine to your table.

4 eggs
2 tablespoons water
1/2 teaspoon garlic salt
1/2 teaspoon chili powder
1/8 teaspoon pepper
1 tablespoon vegetable oil

1 (6-oz.) pkg. frozen avocado dip, thawed
Dash hot pepper sauce
1 tomato, peeled and chopped
1/4 cup dairy sour cream
1 tablespoon vegetable oil

In a small bowl, combine eggs, water, garlic salt, chili powder and pepper. Beat with a fork or whisk until mixed well but not frothy. In an 8-inch omelet pan or skillet, heat 1 tablespoon oil over medium-high heat. When a drop of water sizzles in the pan, pour in half the egg mixture. Cook, gently lifting edges so uncooked portion flows underneath, until eggs are set. In a small bowl, mix avocado dip and hot pepper sauce. Spread half the avocado dip on omelet. Sprinkle with half the chopped tomato and top with half the sour cream. Roll up. Remove from pan. Repeat with 1 tablespoon oil and remaining egg mixture, avocado dip mixture, tomato and sour cream. Makes 2 servings.

Fresh Spring Omelet

Fresh is best, but canned asparagus tips will work just as well.

1 tablespoon vegetable oil	1 tablespoon milk
1/4 cup cooked asparagus tips	1/4 teaspoon celery salt
1/4 cup fresh mushroom slices	Dash pepper
2 teaspoons snipped fresh dillweed, or	1 tablespoon vegetable oil
1/2 teaspoon dried dillweed	1/4 cup shredded sharp Cheddar cheese
2 eggs	

Heat 1 tablespoon oil in a small skillet. Add asparagus, mushrooms and dillweed. Cook and stir until heated through. Remove from heat; keep warm. In a small bowl, combine eggs, milk, celery salt and pepper. Beat with a fork or whisk until mixed well but not frothy. In an 8-inch omelet pan or skillet, heat 1 tablespoon oil over medium-high heat. When a drop of water sizzles in the pan, pour in egg mixture. Cook, gently lifting edges so uncooked portion flows underneath, until eggs are set. Spoon asparagus filling onto omelet; roll up. Sprinkle with cheese. Makes 1 serving.

Oriental Omelet

Chinese vegetables add crunchy texture and an exotic flair.

1 (16-oz.) can fancy mixed Chinese	4 eggs
vegetables, undrained	2 tablespoons water
1 tablespoon cornstarch	1/4 teaspoon salt
1 tablespoon soy sauce	Dash pepper
Dash garlic powder	2 tablespoons vegetable oil

Drain Chinese vegetables; reserve 1/2 cup liquid. Place 1/2 can vegetables in a small saucepan; reserve remaining vegetables for another use. In a small bowl, mix cornstarch, soy sauce and garlic powder. Add reserved liquid from Chinese vegetables; mix well. Stir soy mixture into Chinese vegetables; cook and stir over medium-high heat until thickened and bubbly. Remove and keep warm. In a small bowl, combine eggs, water, salt and pepper. Beat with a fork or whisk until mixed well but not frothy. In an 8-inch omelet pan or skillet, heat 1 tablespoon oil over medium-high heat. When a drop of water sizzles in the pan, pour in half the egg mixture. Cook, gently lifting edges so uncooked portion flows underneath, until eggs are set. Spoon half the vegetable filling onto omelet; roll up. Remove from pan. Add remaining oil to pan; repeat with remaining egg mixture and vegetable filling. Makes 2 servings.

Herbed Omelet

If fresh herbs are available, use 3 times the amount of dried herbs called for in this recipe.

1/4 cup dairy sour cream	**1/8 teaspoon salt**
1 teaspoon Dijon-style mustard	**1 teaspoon dried chives**
2 eggs	**1/4 teaspoon dried leaf chervil**
1 tablespoon water	**1 tablespoon vegetable oil**

In a small bowl, mix sour cream and mustard; set aside. In another small bowl, combine eggs, water, salt, chives and chervil. Beat with a fork or whisk until mixed well but not frothy. Heat oil in an 8-inch omelet pan or skillet over medium-high heat. When a drop of water sizzles in the pan, pour in egg mixture. Cook, gently lifting edges so uncooked portion flows underneath, until eggs are set. Spoon sour cream filling onto omelet; roll up. Makes 1 serving.

Omelet Lorraine

Quiche Lorraine—without the pie crust!

2 slices bacon	**1 tablespoon dried minced onion flakes**
1/4 cup shredded Gruyere or Swiss cheese	**1 tablespoon milk**
1 teaspoon dried parsley flakes	**1/8 teaspoon salt**
2 eggs	**Dash pepper**

Cook bacon in an 8-inch omelet pan or skillet until crisp. Drain, reserving drippings in pan. Crumble bacon and mix in a small bowl with cheese and parsley flakes; set aside. In another small bowl, combine eggs, onion flakes, milk, salt and pepper. Beat with a fork or whisk until mixed well but not frothy. Heat reserved drippings over medium-high heat. When a drop of water sizzles in the pan, pour in egg mixture. Cook, gently lifting edges so uncooked portion flows underneath, until eggs are set. Spoon bacon mixture onto omelet; roll up. Makes 1 serving.

Country Scrambler

Make a delicious midnight supper with toast and jam on the side.

3 slices bacon	**2 tablespoons chopped pimiento**
2 tablespoons chopped onion	**2 tablespoons milk**
2 tablespoons chopped green pepper	**2 oz. American cheese, cut in 1/4-inch cubes**
3 eggs	**(1/2 cup)**

Cook bacon in an 8-inch omelet pan or skillet. Drain; reserve 2 tablespoons drippings in pan. Crumble bacon and set aside. Cook and stir onion and green pepper in reserved drippings until just tender. In a small bowl, combine eggs, pimiento and milk. Beat with a fork or whisk until mixed well but not frothy. Pour into pan. Cook, stirring occasionally, until eggs are almost set. Stir in crumbled bacon and cheese. Cook and stir until eggs are set. Makes 2 servings.

Ham & Eggs in a Hole

Everyone—from toddlers through teens and grandparents—enjoys this fun meal.

2 slices rye bread
1 (2-1/4-oz.) can deviled ham spread
1/2 teaspoon prepared mustard

1 tablespoon vegetable oil
2 eggs
1/4 cup shredded process American cheese

Cut a small circle from the center of each bread slice with center of doughnut cutter or a small lid. Mix ham spread and mustard in a small bowl; set aside. Add oil to a preheated skillet. Place bread slices in skillet. Break 1 egg into hole in each bread slice. Cook until eggs are set. Turn gently. Spread ham mixture on bread around egg and sprinkle with cheese. Cook until ham spread is heated and egg is done as desired. Makes 2 servings.

How to Make Ham & Eggs in a Hole

Cut a hole in bread slices. Break an egg into a custard cup. Place bread in a greased skillet. Carefully pour egg into hole in the bread so yolk is in the center.

Hurry-Up Egg Suppers

- Cook frozen spinach souffle according to package directions. Spoon the cooked souffle onto toasted English muffins. Top each muffin with a poached egg and a spoonful of sour cream with chives. Serve at once.

- Top toast with crisp bacon, tomato slices and a fried egg. Sprinkle with shredded Cheddar cheese and snipped parsley. Let stand a few seconds to soften the cheese.

- Toast a corn muffin round. Top with a fried egg, avocado slices and heated taco sauce. Sprinkle with canned chopped green chilies. Serve hot.

Huevos Rancheros

Serve this Mexican favorite for a late night buffet.

2 tablespoons vegetable oil   **1/4 cup chopped onion**
2 (6-inch) corn tortillas   **1/4 cup chopped green pepper**
2 eggs   **1/2 cup taco sauce**
1 tablespoon vegetable oil   **1/4 cup shredded Cheddar cheese**

Heat 2 tablespoons oil in a medium skillet. Use tongs to hold 1 tortilla at a time in hot oil, cooking until crisp, about 1 minute on each side. Remove and keep warm. Break egg into skillet. Cook until set. Turn and continue cooking until done as desired. Place on top of crisp tortillas and keep warm. Heat 1 tablespoon oil in skillet. Cook and stir onion and green pepper in oil until tender. Stir in taco sauce. Cook and stir until heated through. Spoon sauce over eggs and tortillas. Sprinkle with cheese. Makes 2 servings.

How to Make Huevos Rancheros

Place a fried egg on each crisp tortilla. Spoon taco sauce mixture over eggs. Top with shredded cheese.

Egg Cookery Know-How

Eggs provide very good quality protein at relatively low cost. When appearance rates high, for example in fried eggs, buy Grade A eggs. However, for baking and scrambling, save a few cents and buy Grade B eggs. Buy medium eggs only when a dozen medium eggs is 7 cents cheaper than a dozen large eggs—otherwise large eggs are a better buy. Store eggs covered with their small ends down. Eggs left at room temperature loose their freshness and nutritive quality faster than you realize. Refrigerate them as soon as possible.

Granola Crunch Pancakes

Crush granola between sheets of waxed paper with a rolling pin.

2 cups regular pancake mix　　　　**Vegetable oil**
Milk　　　　　　　　　　　　　　**1 cup crushed granola**
Egg

Prepare pancake batter with milk, egg and oil according to package directions. Brush preheated griddle with oil. Using 1/4 cup batter for each pancake, pour onto griddle. Sprinkle each pancake with 2 tablespoons granola. Cook until underside is golden brown and surface is bubbly. Turn and cook until other side is golden brown. Makes 7 or 8 pancakes.

Variations

Blueberry Pancakes: Substitute 1 cup fresh, thawed frozen, or drained canned blueberries and 1 tablespoon sugar for the granola.
Pineapple Pancakes: Substitute 1 (8-oz.) can drained crushed pineapple for the granola.
Apple-Cinnamon Pancakes: Substitute 1 cup thinly sliced, peeled, cored apple with 1 tablespoon sugar and 1 teaspoon ground cinnamon for the granola.
Spiced Peach Pancakes: Substitute 1 cup chopped canned spiced peaches for the granola.
Cranberry Pancakes: Substitute 1 cup chopped cranberries and 2 tablespoons sugar for granola.

Applesauce Pancakes

To use a complete pancake mix requiring only water, see the variation below.

1 cup regular pancake mix　　　　**1/3 cup applesauce**
1 tablespoon sugar　　　　　　　**1 tablespoon vegetable oil**
1 teaspoon ground cinnamon　　　**Vegetable oil**
1 egg　　　　　　　　　　　　　**Applesauce, if desired**
3/4 cup milk　　　　　　　　　　**Cinnamon-sugar, if desired**

In a medium bowl, mix pancake mix, sugar and cinnamon. Add egg, milk, 1/3 cup applesauce and 1 tablespoon oil. Beat with a whisk until fairly smooth; some lumps will remain. Brush a pre-heated griddle with oil. Using 1/4 cup batter for each pancake, cook on griddle until underside is golden brown and surface is bubbly. Turn and cook until other side is golden brown. Top with applesauce and cinnamon-sugar, if desired. Makes 8 pancakes.

Variation

To use a complete pancake mix that already contains egg, milk and shortening, omit the egg, milk and 1 tablespoon oil. Combine pancake mix with the sugar and cinnamon. Add 3/4 cup water and 1/3 cup applesauce. Mix and bake as directed above.

Blueberry-Lemon Pancakes

Lemon yogurt gives blueberry pancakes magnificent texture and delectable flavor.

1 cup all-purpose flour
2 tablespoons sugar
1 tablespoon baking powder
1/2 teaspoon salt
1/4 teaspoon baking soda
1 egg, beaten
1/2 cup milk
1/2 cup lemon yogurt

2 tablespoons vegetable oil
Vegetable oil
1 cup fresh, thawed frozen or
    drained canned blueberries
1/2 cup lemon yogurt
1/4 cup fresh, thawed frozen or
    drained canned blueberries

In a medium bowl, mix flour, sugar, baking powder, salt and baking soda. In a small bowl, combine egg, milk, 1/2 cup lemon yogurt and 2 tablespoons oil. Add to flour mixture. Beat with a whisk until fairly smooth; some lumps will remain. Brush a preheated griddle with oil. Using 1/4 cup batter for each pancake, pour onto griddle. Sprinkle with 2 tablespoons blueberries on each pancake. Cook until underside is golden brown and surface is bubbly. Turn and cook until other side is golden brown. To serve, top with remaining yogurt and garnish with remaining blueberries. Makes 8 pancakes.

Peach Melba Pancakes

Invite a friend over after the movies for a memorable supper.

1 (8-oz.) can peach slices, undrained
1 cup regular pancake mix
1 tablespoon sugar
Milk
Egg

Vegetable oil
1 (10-oz.) pkg. frozen sweetened raspberries,
    thawed
1 cup whipped topping

Drain peaches; reserve 2 tablespoons syrup. Chop peach slices into small pieces. In a medium bowl, mix pancake mix and sugar. Prepare pancake batter with milk, egg and oil according to package directions, substituting the peach syrup for 2 tablespoons of the milk. Gently stir in chopped peaches. Brush a preheated griddle with oil. Using 1/4 cup batter for each pancake, cook on griddle until underside is golden brown and surface is bubbly. Turn and cook until other side is golden brown. Top with raspberries and a dollop of whipped topping. Makes 7 or 8 pancakes.

Blueberry Lemon Pancakes

Peanut Butter & Jelly Stack-Ups

Also a wonderful treat for breakfast or brunch.

1 cup regular pancake mix	**1/3 cup chunk-style peanut butter**
1 tablespoon sugar	**1-1/2 cups grape jelly**
Milk	**About 2 tablespoons chunk-style**
Egg	** peanut butter**
Vegetable oil	**1/4 cup chopped peanuts**

In a medium bowl, combine pancake mix and sugar. Prepare pancake batter with milk, egg and oil according to package directions, adding 1/3 cup peanut butter with the liquid called for on the package. Brush preheated griddle with oil. Using 1/4 cup batter for each pancake, cook on griddle until underside is golden brown and surface is bubbly. Turn and cook until other side is golden brown. Use 4 pancakes for each stack. Spread jelly on 3 pancakes and cover with fourth pancake. Spread top with peanut butter. Add a dollop of jelly and sprinkle with peanuts. Makes 2 servings.

How to Make Peanut Butter & Jelly Stack-Ups

1/Let the youngsters choose their favorite jelly for spreading on the pancakes.

2/Stack them as high as you like—then top them with more peanut butter, jelly and peanuts.

1/Cut a pocket in each thick bread slice, then spoon in strawberry preserves and chopped pecans.

2/Dip the bread in egg mixture. Cook until golden brown. Top with powdered sugar and fresh strawberries.

How to Make Strawberry French Toast

Strawberry French Toast

You'll need an uncut loaf of bread to cut slices thick enough for making pockets.

2 slices bread, cut 1 inch thick
3 tablespoons strawberry preserves
1 tablespoon chopped pecans
1 egg, slightly beaten
1/3 cup milk

1-1/2 teaspoons sugar
1/4 teaspoon vanilla extract
2 tablespoons butter or margarine
2 tablespoons powdered sugar
1/4 cup fresh strawberries

Cut pocket in 1 end of each bread slice, cutting to other end but not through. In a small bowl, mix strawberry preserves and pecans. Stuff half the mixture into each pocket. In a pie plate, mix egg, milk, sugar and vanilla. Melt butter or margarine on a preheated griddle. Carefully dip both sides of bread slices into egg mixture. Cook on buttered griddle until one side is browned. Turn and sprinkle with half the powdered sugar. Cook until other side is browned. Turn and sprinkle with remaining powdered sugar. Top with strawberries. Makes 2 servings.

Waffles with Creamed Sausage

You can also spoon the creamy sauce over broiled tomato halves or broccoli spears.

12 oz. bulk pork sausage
1/4 cup sliced green onion
1/4 cup all-purpose flour
2-1/2 cups milk

1 (3-oz.) can sliced mushrooms, drained
1 (2-oz.) jar pimiento, drained, chopped
1/2 cup dairy sour cream
6 frozen waffles, toasted

In a large skillet, cook sausage and green onion over medium-high heat until sausage is browned, stirring occasionally. Drain off drippings. Sprinkle flour over sausage mixture; stir to blend. Add milk. Stir constantly over medium-high heat until thickened and bubbly. Add mushrooms and pimiento. Stir a small amount of hot mixture into sour cream. Add sour cream mixture to hot mixture; stir to blend. Keep warm while toasting waffles but *do not boil*. Serve creamed mixture over toasted waffles. Makes 6 servings.

Ham & Egg Crepes with Creamy Onion Sauce

Frozen crepes are available in some supermarkets, gourmet shops and bakeries.

2 tablespoons butter or margarine
8 eggs, slightly beaten
1 cup diced cooked ham
1 (3-oz.) can sliced mushrooms, drained
1/4 cup milk
1 teaspoon snipped chives

1/4 teaspoon salt
1/8 teaspoon pepper
6 frozen crepes (about 6-1/2 inches
  in diameter)
Creamy Onion Sauce, see below

Creamy Onion Sauce:
1 (9-oz.) pkg. frozen onions in cream sauce
1 teaspoon dried parsley flakes

2 tablespoons grated Parmesan cheese

Grease a 12" x 7" baking dish. Preheat oven to 375°F (190°C). Melt butter or margarine in a medium skillet. In a medium bowl, mix eggs, ham, mushrooms, milk, chives, salt and pepper. Pour egg mixture into skillet. Cook until eggs are set, stirring occasionally. Remove from heat. Spoon about 1/3 cup egg mixture onto each crepe. Roll up and place seam-side up in greased baking dish. Prepare Creamy Onion Sauce. Pour sauce over crepes. Cover and bake 20 to 25 minutes or until heated through. Serve immediately. Makes 6 servings.

Creamy Onion Sauce:
In a small saucepan, prepare onions according to package directions. Stir in parsley flakes and Parmesan cheese. Makes 1-1/3 cups of sauce.

Saucy Pizza Wedges

Ready-to-use pizza crusts are in supermarkets on the shelf and in the refrigerator case.

1 (7-oz.) can luncheon meat
8 oz. ground beef
1/4 teaspoon salt
1/4 teaspoon dried rubbed sage
1/4 teaspoon dried leaf oregano

1 (8-oz.) can pizza sauce
1 10- to 12-inch ready-to-bake pizza crust
**1 (4-oz.) pkg. shredded mozzarella cheese
   (1 cup)**

Preheat oven to 425°F (220°C). Chop canned luncheon meat into small pieces. In a medium skillet, mix chopped luncheon meat and ground beef. Stir over medium-high heat until lightly browned. Drain off excess fat. Stir in salt, sage, oregano, and pizza sauce. Spoon onto pizza crust in a 12-inch pizza pan. Top with shredded cheese. Bake 13 to 15 minutes or until crust is browned and filling is bubbly. Cut into wedges. Makes one 10- to 12-inch pizza.

How to Make Saucy Pizza Wedges

1/Stir pizza sauce and herbs into browned meats. Spoon onto a ready-to-bake pizza crust.

2/Sprinkle pizza generously with mozzarella cheese. Bake about 15 minutes. Cut in large wedges.

Salmon Stratas

Tartar sauce and lemon juice add a pleasant tang to individual salmon stratas.

1-1/2 cups herb-seasoned croutons	1/2 teaspoon lemon juice
1 (7-oz.) can salmon, drained, chunked	1/2 cup shredded Cheddar cheese
1/2 cup frozen peas, thawed	1 egg, slightly beaten
1/4 cup bottled tartar sauce	1 (5-1/3 oz.) can evaporated milk (2/3 cup)

Butter two 2-cup baking dishes. Place 1/2 cup croutons in each baking dish. Mix salmon and peas in a medium bowl. Fold in tartar sauce and lemon juice. Spoon half the salmon mixture into each prepared baking dish. Top with Cheddar cheese and remaining croutons. Combine egg and evaporated milk in a small bowl. Beat with a fork or whisk until mixed well but not frothy. Pour over croutons. Cover and refrigerate 2 to 24 hours. Preheat oven to 375°F (190°C). Bake casseroles uncovered 30 minutes or until set. Let stand 5 minutes. Makes 2 servings.

Steak Slices Supreme

You'll be proud of this beautiful make-ahead steak sandwich platter.

1 (1- to 1-1/2-lb.) beef flank steak	2 tablespoons vegetable oil
1/3 cup soy sauce	Parsley sprigs or watercress
1/3 cup rum	Pumpernickel bread slices, halved, buttered

Trim any excess fat from steak. Place in a shallow baking dish. Combine soy sauce and rum; pour over steak. Cover and refrigerate overnight, turning steak occasionally in marinade. Preheat broiler to medium temperature. Place steak on rack of broiler pan; brush with 1 tablespoon oil. Broil 3 inches from heat 5 minutes; turn and brush with remaining oil. Broil 5 minutes longer or until medium-rare. Place steak in another shallow baking dish. Pour pan juices over steak; cool. Cover and chill. To serve, use a sharp knife to cut thin diagonal slices. Arrange on a plate. Garnish with parsley or watercress. Serve buttered bread slices separately. Makes 6 to 8 servings.

Confetti Ham Foldovers

A delicious combination for either a late supper or special luncheon.

1 (7-oz.) pkg. frozen rice and peas with mushrooms, cooked, drained	3 tablespoons creamy green goddess salad dressing
2 tablespoons grated Parmesan cheese	4 thin rectangular ham slices
2 tablespoons drained chopped canned pimiento	2 slices American cheese, halved diagonally
Dash pepper	Snipped fresh parsley
	Paprika

Preheat oven to 375°F (190°C). In a medium bowl, combine cooked rice mixture, Parmesan cheese, pimiento and pepper. Gently mix in salad dressing. Spoon about 1/2 cup rice filling on half of each ham slice. Fold over other half. Carefully place in a 10" x 6" baking dish. Cover with foil. Bake 15 to 20 minutes or until heated. Arrange cheese on foldovers. Bake 3 to 4 minutes to melt cheese. Sprinkle with parsley and paprika. Makes 4 servings.

No-Fuss Salads & Vegetables

Crisp salads or relishes and crisp-tender vegetables can provide texture and flavor contrasts in almost any meal. If you shop every day, crisp green salads are no problem. But if you are limited to one shopping trip a week, the fresh vegetables you buy need special attention to keep them fresh.

Thoroughly rinse and drain salad greens as soon as you unpack them from the shopping bag. Let them drain on paper towels. Fold two or three paper towels and place them in the bottom of a large plastic bag. Gently place the drained greens on the paper towels without crowding them. Close the bag tightly and keep it in the refrigerator. When you're ready to make a salad, the greens will already be washed and crisped.

Treat celery as you would greens. Separate the stalks before rinsing, then trim to desired lengths. After draining on paper towels, place the celery pieces in a plastic bag with paper towels. Celery sticks will be ready and waiting whenever you need them for a salad or relish tray.

Fresh parsley gives a quick salad plate a distinguished look. Rinse parsley before you refrigerate it. Break off the long stems and shake excess water from the leaves. Pat with paper towels to absorb remaining excess water. Place the parsley in a 2-quart jar or large plastic container but do not pack down. Cover the container tightly and store it in the refrigerator. This way you can keep parsley up to one week.

Salads and vegetables need very little imagination to give them special touches. Here are a few ideas to help you create interesting vegetable dishes and salads with almost no fuss:

● Shake up a new salad dressing combination. Match bottled French dressing with blue cheese dressing, creamy cucumber with creamy Italian, Thousand Island with green goddess, or creamy onion with bacon dressing.

● Use mixed salad greens instead of just lettuce. If you're a gardener, toss in the first tender leaves of beets, nasturtiums and spinach that you thin out of the rows.

● Add crunch to vegetables or salads with flavored croutons, canned French fried onions, crumbled crisp bacon, chow mein noodles, rice noodles or water chestnuts.

● Sauté chopped onion in butter. Stir in a sprinkling of celery salt, basil and thyme. Drizzle the onion-herb butter over your favorite green vegetable.

● Fill tomato halves or large mushroom caps with thawed frozen spinach soufflé. Sprinkle with Parmesan cheese and bake until heated through.

● Spread hot cooked cauliflower or broccoli with sour cream dip and sprinkle with shredded cheese.

A colorful buffet supper of tempting salads and vegetables is pictured on the following pages. Clockwise from top right: Potatoes with Creamy Baked Potato Topping, page 101; Stir-Fry Medley, page 98; California Salad Toss, page 91; Asparagus Vinaigrette Salad, page 91; Party Pink Salad Freeze, page 95.

Naturally Good Salad

When you buy sunflower seeds for cooking, be sure the shells are removed.

4 cups torn leaf lettuce	**2 tablespoons sunflower seeds**
1/2 cup mung bean sprouts	**1 tablespoon lemon juice**
1/2 cup shredded Cheddar cheese	**1 teaspoon honey**
1/4 cup shredded carrot	**1/4 teaspoon dry mustard**
1 tablespoon butter or margarine	**1/8 teaspoon dried dillweed**
1/2 cup croutons	**2 tablespoons vegetable oil**

In a salad bowl, mix lettuce, bean sprouts, cheese and carrot. Cover tightly and refrigerate until serving time. Melt butter or margarine in a small skillet. Add croutons and sunflower seeds. Toss over medium heat until toasted; set aside. In a small container with a tight-fitting lid, mix lemon juice, honey, dry mustard and dillweed; shake well. Add oil. Shake again; chill. To serve, shake dressing and pour over salad. Add croutons and sunflower seeds; toss. Makes 3 or 4 servings.

Ambrosia Slaw

If you don't have a food processor, shred cabbage with a large sharp knife.

1/2 (11-oz.) can mandarin orange sections, drained	**2 tablespoons flaked coconut**
1 (8-oz.) can pineapple chunks, drained	**1/4 cup whipped topping**
1/2 cup miniature marshmallows	**1/4 cup pineapple yogurt**
	1-1/2 cups shredded cabbage

In a medium bowl, mix mandarin orange sections, pineapple chunks, marshmallows and coconut. In a small bowl, mix whipped topping and pineapple yogurt. Fold whipped topping mixture into fruit mixture. Stir in cabbage. Refrigerate until serving time. Makes 4 servings.

Wilted Spinach Salad

For more variety, substitute fresh leaf lettuce for the spinach or add sautéed mushrooms.

4 slices bacon	**1/4 teaspoon salt**
2 tablespoons chopped green onion	**Dash pepper**
1/4 cup red wine vinegar	**1/2 (10-oz.) pkg. fresh spinach, washed, stems removed**
2 tablespoons water	**2 hard-cooked eggs, sliced**
1 teaspoon sugar	**1 tomato, peeled, quartered**
1 teaspoon Worcestershire sauce	
1/2 teaspoon dry mustard	

Cook bacon in a medium skillet until crisp. Drain; reserve drippings in skillet. Crumble bacon and set aside. Cook and stir green onion in drippings until tender. Stir in vinegar, water, sugar, Worcestershire sauce, dry mustard, salt, pepper and crumbled bacon. Bring to a boil, stirring occasionally. In a salad bowl, mix spinach, hard-cooked eggs and tomato. Pour hot dressing over salad; toss. Makes 4 servings.

Asparagus Vinaigrette Salad   Photo on pages 88 and 89.

In the oh-so-short fresh asparagus season, substitute fresh asparagus for frozen.

1 (10-oz.) pkg. frozen asparagus spears
Water
1/2 cup vegetable oil
1/3 cup white wine vinegar
1 envelope Italian salad dressing mix
3 tablespoons chopped green pepper

3 tablespoons chopped radishes
1 tablespoon snipped fresh parsley
1 tablespoon snipped chives
1 head Boston lettuce
4 thick tomato slices
4 pimiento strips

In a small skillet, cook asparagus in water according to package directions; drain. Set aside in a shallow baking dish. In a small container with a tight-fitting lid, mix oil, vinegar and salad dressing mix; shake well. Add green pepper, radishes, parsley and chives; shake well. Pour over asparagus. Cover and refrigerate 4 to 24 hours. Drain; reserve marinade. Line 4 salad plates with lettuce. Place a tomato slice on lettuce. Top with asparagus. Gather asparagus into a bundle. Arrange pimiento strips to look like ties for bundles. Drizzle with dressing. Makes 4 servings.

Make-Ahead Salad Toss

A super salad combination, a deluxe dressing, and you made it yesterday!

1/2 large head iceberg lettuce,
    torn in bite-size pieces
6 cherry tomatoes, halved
3 hard-cooked eggs, sliced
Dash salt and pepper
1/2 small cucumber, peeled, seeded, sliced
2 tablespoons chopped green onion

2 tablespoons chopped green pepper
1 cup shredded Cheddar cheese (4 oz.)
1/2 (4-oz.) carton semi-soft natural
    cheese with garlic and herbs
1/3 cup cucumber salad dressing
2 tablespoons imitation bacon bits

Layer half the lettuce in a salad bowl. Add tomatoes, egg slices, salt and pepper. Add cucumber, green onion, green pepper and remaining lettuce. Sprinkle with Cheddar cheese. In a small bowl, mix natural cheese with salad dressing. Spread over salad, sealing to sides of bowl. Cover; refrigerate up to 24 hours. To serve, sprinkle with bacon bits; toss. Makes 6 servings.

California Salad Toss   Photo on pages 88 and 89.

If the salad must wait in the refrigerator, brush the avocado slices with lemon juice to prevent darkening.

6 cups torn romaine lettuce
1 orange, peeled, sectioned
1 grapefruit, peeled, sectioned
1 avocado, peeled, seeded, sliced

1 small red onion, sliced, separated in rings
1 cup fresh mushroom slices
1/4 cup orange yogurt
1/4 cup creamy French dressing

Place lettuce in a large salad bowl. Add orange, grapefruit, avocado, onion, and mushrooms. In a small bowl, combine yogurt and dressing; mix well. Drizzle over salad; toss. Makes 6 servings.

Four-Way Salad Dressing

This recipe provides the base for four dressings.

2 cups mayonnaise or mayonnaise-style
   salad dressing

2 cups dairy sour cream

Mix mayonnaise or salad dressing and sour cream in a medium bowl. Turn into a covered container; refrigerate. Use by itself or as a base for Zesty Guacamole Dressing, Tropical Fruit Dressing, Creamy Goddess Dressing and Russian Dressing. Makes 4 cups of dressing.

Creamy Goddess Dressing

A delightfully flavored dressing with a smooth creamy base is perfect for mixed salad greens.

1 cup Four-Way Salad Dressing, above
1/4 cup snipped fresh parsley
1/4 cup snipped fresh watercress

2 tablespoons tarragon vinegar
1 tablespoon anchovy paste
1 tablespoon snipped fresh chives

In blender, combine salad dressing, parsley, watercress, vinegar, anchovy paste and chives. Cover and process on high speed 1 minute or until smooth. Makes 1-1/4 cups of dressing.

How to Make & Use Four-Way Salad Dressing

1/Fold together mayonnaise and sour cream. Cover and refrigerate. Use as a base for other salad dressings.

2/Garnish Zesty Guacamole Dressing with avocado slices. Sprinkle Tropical Fruit Dressing with shredded orange peel. Top Russian Dressing with hard-cooked egg slices.

Zesty Guacamole Dressing

Spoon this thick dressing over red ripe tomato slices on lettuce leaves.

1 cup Four-Way Salad Dressing, page 92
1 avocado, peeled, cut up
3 to 4 tablespoons canned chopped
  green chilies

2 tablespoons lemon juice
1/2 teaspoon onion salt
Avocado slices

In blender, combine salad dressing, avocado pieces, chilies, lemon juice and onion salt. Cover and process on high speed 1 minute or until smooth. Chill. Garnish with avocado slices. Makes 1-1/2 cups of dressing.

Tropical Fruit Dressing

Ladle this creamy dressing over canned or fresh fruits.

1 cup Four-Way Salad Dressing, page 92
3 tablespoons thawed frozen pineapple
  juice concentrate
2 tablespoons powdered sugar

1/2 teaspoon grated orange peel
Dash ground allspice
Grated orange peel

In a small bowl, combine salad dressing, pineapple juice concentrate, sugar, 1/2 teaspoon orange peel and allspice; mix well. Chill. Garnish with orange peel. Makes 1 cup of dressing.

Russian Dressing

Whether you call it Russian or Thousand Island, it's delicious on crisp lettuce wedges.

1 cup Four-Way Salad Dressing, page 92
1/3 cup chili sauce
2 hard-cooked eggs, chopped
1/3 cup pickle relish

1/3 cup chopped green pepper
2 teaspoons instant minced onion
Hard-cooked egg slices

In a small bowl, mix salad dressing, chili sauce, chopped hard-cooked eggs, pickle relish, green pepper and onion. Stir to mix well. Chill. Before serving, garnish with hard-cooked egg slices. Makes 2-1/3 cups of dressing.

Hot German Potato Salad

Tangy potato salad with sandwiches or burgers is a treat for a summer evening.

3 slices bacon
1/2 cup chopped onion
2 teaspoons all-purpose flour
1/2 cup water
2 tablespoons cider vinegar
4 teaspoons sugar

1 tablespoon snipped fresh parsley
1/4 teaspoon salt
1 (16-oz.) can potatoes, drained, sliced
   1/4 inch thick
2 tablespoons chopped pimiento

Cook bacon in a medium skillet until crisp. Drain; reserve drippings in skillet. Crumble bacon and set aside. Cook and stir onion in bacon drippings until tender. Stir in flour. Add water, vinegar, sugar, parsley and salt. Cook and stir until mixture thickens and boils. Add potatoes, pimiento and bacon. Toss gently and heat through. Makes 2 or 3 servings.

Easiest Vegetable Salad

Pour sauce over mixed vegetables for a simple but delicious salad.

1 (10-oz.) pkg. frozen mixed vegetables,
   cooked, drained
1/4 cup Italian salad dressing
1/4 cup mayonnaise or mayonnaise-style
   salad dressing

2 tablespoons chili sauce
1 hard-cooked egg, finely chopped
Dash salt and pepper
Chopped lettuce

Place hot vegetables in a medium bowl. Add Italian salad dressing; toss. Cover and chill. In a small bowl, combine mayonnaise, chili sauce, egg, salt and pepper; mix well. To serve, drain vegetables. Arrange lettuce on 4 salad plates. Spoon vegetables on top of lettuce. Drizzle mayonaise mixture over vegetables. Makes 4 servings.

Pickled Peaches   *Photo on pages 4 and 5.*

Keep these spicy peaches in your refrigerator for a spur-of-the-moment relish.

1 (29-oz.) can peach halves
Whole cloves
1/2 cup sugar

1/2 cup white wine vinegar
1 (2-inch) cinnamon stick

Drain peaches; reserve 1 cup peach syrup. Cut each peach half in half again. Stud each piece with 2 cloves. Place peaches in a medium bowl and set aside. In a medium saucepan, mix reserved peach syrup, sugar and vinegar. Add cinnamon stick. Bring to a boil; reduce heat. Simmer uncovered until sugar is dissolved. Pour syrup over peaches. Cover and refrigerate overnight or up to several weeks. Makes about 1 quart of pickled peaches.

Easy Fruit Salad

Here's a recipe that gives you a fruit salad for supper and dessert for tomorrow's lunch.

1 (3-3/4-oz.) pkg. instant vanilla
    pudding mix
1-1/2 cups milk
1/2 (6-oz.) can thawed frozen pineapple-
    orange juice concentrate (1/3 cup)
1 (8-oz.) carton pineapple-orange yogurt

1 (8-oz.) can sliced peaches, drained, chilled
1-1/2 cups sliced fresh strawberries, chilled
1 cup fresh blueberries, chilled
1 cup seedless green grapes, chilled
1 large banana, peeled, sliced

In a large bowl, beat pudding mix, milk and pineapple-orange concentrate with electric mixer on low speed 2 minutes. Beat in yogurt by hand. Reserve half the mixture to serve as pudding. In another large bowl, mix peaches, strawberries, blueberries, grapes and bananas. Fold in remaining half of the pudding mixture. Cover and refrigerate 2 hours but not longer than 4 hours or mixture may become soupy. Makes 5 or 6 servings.

Party Pink Salad Freeze   *Photo on pages 88 and 89.*

No thawing time required—cut this salad in squares right from the freezer.

1 (21-oz.) can cherry pie filling
1 (14-oz.) can sweetened condensed milk
1 (8-1/4-oz.) can crushed pineapple,
    drained
1/4 cup chopped pecans
1/4 cup lemon juice

Few drops red food coloring, if desired
1 (4-oz.) carton frozen whipped topping,
    thawed
Endive leaves
Additional whipped topping
Fresh cherries

In a medium bowl, combine pie filling, sweetened condensed milk, pineapple, pecans and lemon juice. Add food coloring, if desired. Mix well. Fold in whipped topping. Turn into a 10'' x 6'' baking dish. Cover and freeze until firm. Cut in 6 to 8 squares. Serve on endive leaves. Garnish with additional whipped topping and fresh cherries. Makes 6 to 8 servings.

Fancy Tossed Salad

Marinade from the jar of artichoke hearts is used for the dressing.

1 (6-oz.) jar marinated artichoke hearts,
    undrained
1 cup sliced fresh mushrooms

4 cups torn salad greens
1 tablespoon lemon juice
1/2 to 1 teaspoon salad seasoning

Place undrained artichoke hearts in a medium salad bowl. Add mushrooms. Mix gently to coat mushrooms with marinade. Place salad greens on top of mushrooms. Cover tightly and refrigerate. Before serving, sprinkle with lemon juice and salad seasoning; toss gently. Makes 4 servings.

Herb-Fried Tomatoes

To be suitable for frying, tomatoes should be either green and mature or red but still firm.

1 large, firm tomato, sliced 1/4 inch thick
Salt and pepper
1 cup herb-seasoned breadcrumbs for
   stuffing, finely crushed

1 egg, beaten
2 tablespoons vegetable oil
Shredded Cheddar cheese

Sprinkle tomato slices with salt and pepper. Place breadcrumbs and egg in 2 separate pie plates. Dip tomato slices in breadcrumbs, then in egg, then again in breadcrumbs. Heat oil in a large skillet. Cook tomato slices in hot oil until golden brown on one side. Turn and cook until golden brown on second side. Top with shredded Cheddar cheese. Makes 2 servings.

Elegant Green Beans

The cream cheese topping is also wonderful with broccoli and asparagus.

3 slices bacon
1 (16-oz.) can green beans
1 (3-oz.) pkg. cream cheese, softened

1 tablespoon milk
1/2 teaspoon dried dillweed

Cook bacon in a medium skillet until crisp. Drain; reserve drippings in skillet. Crumble bacon and set aside. Drain green beans; reserve 1/4 cup liquid. Add reserved bean liquid and green beans to drippings in skillet. Cook until heated through. In a small bowl, mix crumbled bacon, cream cheese, milk and dillweed. Stir until no cream cheese lumps remain. Spoon over green beans. Makes 3 servings.

Pea Pods & Rice

Undercook rather than overcook the vegetables so they retain their crispness.

2 tablespoons butter or margarine
2 tablespoons chopped onion
1 cup sliced fresh mushrooms

1 (6-oz.) pkg. frozen pea pods
1 to 2 teaspoons soy sauce
1 cup cooked rice

Melt butter or margarine in a medium skillet. Add onion and mushrooms. Cook until barely tender. Add pea pods. Cook and stir over high heat until pea pods are crisp-tender. Add soy sauce and rice; toss gently. Heat through, stirring frequently. Serve at once. Makes 4 servings.

Fiery Potato Bake

Reduce the amount of chilies if you can't take the heat.

Instant mashed potatoes to make 4 servings
Water
Milk
Salt
Butter

1/2 cup shredded Cheddar cheese
1/2 cup dairy sour cream
3 to 4 tablespoons drained canned chopped
  green chilies
1/2 teaspoon dried parsley flakes

Preheat oven to 350°F (175°C). Prepare instant mashed potatoes with water, milk, salt and butter according to package directions. Stir in Cheddar cheese, sour cream and chopped chilies. Turn into a 1-quart casserole. Sprinkle with parsley flakes. Bake 20 minutes or until heated through. Makes 4 servings.

Soy Spinach

Try it with Polynesian Stuffed Bratwurst, page 58.

2 tablespoons vegetable oil
1 tablespoon soy sauce
1/2 teaspoon sugar

1 (10-oz.) pkg. frozen chopped spinach,
  thawed, drained
1/2 cup coarsely chopped water chestnuts

In a medium skillet, combine oil, soy sauce and sugar. Add spinach and water chestnuts. Stir over medium-high heat until heated through. Makes 3 servings.

Cheese-Topped Skillet

Vegetables fresh from the garden are enhanced by herbs and cheese.

4 tablespoons butter or margarine
2 cups fresh broccoli flowerets
1 small onion, very thinly sliced
2 small zucchini, sliced 1/4 inch thick
Salt and pepper
1 tablespoon snipped fresh oregano or
  1/2 teaspoon dried leaf oregano

1 tablespoon snipped fresh basil or
  1/2 teaspoon dried leaf basil
1 tomato, cut in wedges
1 cup shredded process American cheese
  (4 oz.)

Melt butter or margarine in a large skillet. Add broccoli and onion. Cover and cook over medium heat 2 minutes. Add zucchini. Season with salt and pepper. Add oregano and basil. Cover and cook over medium heat 3 minutes or until vegetables are crisp-tender, stirring occasionally. Add tomato. Sprinkle with cheese. Cover and cook 1 to 2 minutes to melt cheese. Makes 4 servings.

Stir-Fry Medley   *Photo on pages 88 and 89.*

Store cut ginger root in your refrigerator in a small jar filled with sherry.

1 tablespoon vegetable oil
1 small yellow summer squash, thinly sliced
1/2 small red or green pepper,
   cut in strips
3 cauliflowerets, thinly sliced
1 carrot, thinly sliced

2 green onions, sliced
1/2 teaspoon garlic salt
1/2 teaspoon grated fresh ginger root
1 tablespoon snipped fresh parsley or
   tarragon

Heat oil in a medium skillet. Add squash, pepper, cauliflowerets, carrot and green onions. Sprinkle with garlic salt and ginger root. Stir over medium-high heat until vegetables are crisp-tender. Spoon onto serving plate and sprinkle with parsley or tarragon. Makes 3 servings.

Best Creamy Beets

Do not boil the sauce or it may develop an unpleasant texture.

1 (16-oz.) can sliced or diced beets
1/4 cup plain yogurt
2 tablespoons mayonnaise or
   mayonnaise-style salad dressing

1 tablespoon finely chopped green onion
1 teaspoon lemon juice
1/4 teaspoon prepared horseradish
Dash salt

Bring beets to a boil in a small saucepan. Remove from heat; drain well. Combine remaining ingredients in a small bowl; mix well. Pour over beets. Cook over low heat until heated through but do not boil. Makes 2 or 3 servings.

Quick Creamed Vegetables

A really fast vegetable dish when you use a homemade sauce stick.

1/8 Parmesan Sauce Stick, page 110, or
   Herbed Sauce Stick, page 111
1/2 cup water

1 (10-oz.) pkg. frozen peas, cut green
   beans, mixed vegetables, baby lima beans,
   chopped broccoli or cut asparagus

Crumble sauce stick into a medium saucepan. Add water and frozen vegetables. Bring to a boil. Break up vegetables with a large fork. Stir to blend sauce; reduce heat. Cover and simmer until vegetables are tender, stirring occasionally. Makes 2 or 3 servings.

Confetti Bake

If you make this casserole the night before, refrigerate it and bake it 10 minutes longer.

1 (10-3/4-oz.) can condensed cream of
    onion soup
1 cup shredded sharp process American
    cheese (4 oz.)
1/2 cup mayonnaise or mayonnaise-style
    salad dressing
1/4 cup milk
1 (10-oz.) pkg. frozen cauliflower,
    cooked, drained

1 (9-oz.) pkg. frozen peas and carrots,
    cooked, drained
1/4 cup pimiento
1 (3-oz.) can sliced mushrooms, drained
3 tablespoons butter or margarine
1/2 cup seasoned dry breadcrumbs
1/4 cup grated Parmesan cheese

Preheat oven to 375°F (190°C). In a large bowl, combine soup, American cheese, mayonnaise or salad dressing and milk; mix well. Gently fold in cauliflower, peas and carrots, pimiento and mushrooms. Turn into 1-1/2-quart baking dish. Melt butter or margarine in a small saucepan. Stir in breadcrumbs and Parmesan cheese. Sprinkle over casserole. Bake uncovered 35 to 45 minutes or until heated through. Makes 6 to 8 servings.

How to Make Confetti Bake

1/Mix canned cream of onion soup, shredded cheese and mayonnaise. Gently fold in cooked vegetables.

2/Sprinkle casserole with buttered breadcrumbs seasoned with Parmesan cheese.

Skillet Potatoes & Cheese

Loosen the potatoes with a spatula before turning them over.

4 large baking potatoes, peeled
4 tablespoons butter or margarine
Onion salt
Celery salt
Pepper

Dash dried dillweed
1 cup shredded sharp process American
  cheese (4 oz.)
1/2 (3-oz.) can French fried onions
Snipped fresh parsley

Slice potatoes 1/4 inch thick. Melt butter or margarine in a large skillet. Layer half the potatoes over bottom of skillet. Sprinkle generously with onion salt, celery salt and pepper. Add dillweed. Repeat potato layer and seasonings. Cover and cook over medium heat 10 minutes. With a wide spatula, carefully turn potatoes over. Cover and cook 10 minutes or until potatoes are tender. Sprinkle with cheese and onions. Remove cover and cook 1 minute or until cheese is melted. Garnish with snipped parsley. Makes 4 servings.

Sweet & Sour Red Cabbage

Red wine vinegar and brown sugar add a piquant flavor to red cabbage.

2 tablespoons butter or margarine
3/4 cup chopped red cabbage
3/4 cup chopped peeled apple
1/4 cup water

2 tablespoons red wine vinegar
1 tablespoon brown sugar
1/2 teaspoon caraway seeds
Salt and pepper

Melt butter or margarine in a medium skillet. Add cabbage and apple. Cook and stir until crisp-tender. In a small bowl, mix water, vinegar, brown sugar and caraway seeds. Stir into cabbage mixture. Cook and stir until heated through. Season with salt and pepper. Makes 3 servings.

Maple-Glazed Carrots

Buttery maple syrup makes sweet tender carrots a real delicacy.

1-1/4 cups frozen carrots
Water
3 tablespoons butter or margarine

3 tablespoons maple-flavored syrup
1/2 teaspoon grated lemon peel
1/8 teaspoon ground mace

In a small saucepan, cook carrots in water according to package directions; drain. Add butter or margarine. In a small bowl or cup, mix maple syrup, lemon peel and mace. Pour over carrots. Cook and stir over medium-high heat until carrots are lightly glazed. Makes 2 or 3 servings.

Vegetarian Fried Rice

Enjoy multi-textured fried rice with your most exotic Oriental dish.

2 tablespoons vegetable oil
1/4 cup mung bean sprouts
2 tablespoons chopped green onion
2 tablespoons chopped green or red pepper
2 tablespoons chopped celery

1/8 teaspoon garlic salt
1/4 cup water
1 teaspoon soy sauce
1/2 (12-oz.) can fried rice

Heat oil in a medium skillet. Add bean sprouts, onion, pepper and celery. Cook and stir over medium-high heat until crisp-tender. Sprinkle with garlic salt. Add water and soy sauce. Stir in rice. Cook until heated through, stirring often. Makes 2 or 3 servings.

Variations

Pork, Chicken or Shrimp Fried Rice: To make a main dish, add about 1/3 cup diced cooked pork, chicken or shrimp with rice.

Creamed Pea Combo

A touch of dry sherry gives this vegetable trio a delicate flavor.

2 tablespoons butter or margarine
1 tablespoon all-purpose flour
3/4 cup milk
1 tablespoon dry sherry
1/2 teaspoon chicken bouillon granules

1 (8-1/2-oz.) can peas, drained
1 (8-oz.) can small whole stewed onions, drained
1 (2-1/2-oz.) jar mushrooms, drained
Salt and pepper

Melt butter or margarine in a medium saucepan. Stir in flour. Add milk, sherry, and chicken bouillon granules. Cook and stir over medium-high heat until thickened and bubbly. Add peas, onions and mushrooms. Heat through. Season with salt and pepper. Makes 3 or 4 servings.

Creamy Baked Potato Topping   *Photo on pages 88 and 89.*

Top split baked potatoes with this cheese topping then garnish them with chives and paprika.

1/2 cup butter or margarine, softened
1 (5-oz.) jar sharp process cheese spread

1 cup dairy sour cream
1 tablespoon snipped fresh chives

In a small mixing bowl, beat softened butter or margarine and cheese spread with electric mixer on high speed until fluffy. Beat in sour cream and chives. Use immediately or cover and chill; remove from refrigerator 1 hour before serving to soften. Makes 2-1/4 cups of topping.

Cheese & Carrot Cakes

The crunchy cashew coating makes carrot-cheese-rice cakes irresistible.

1 cup hot cooked rice
1/2 cup grated carrot
1/2 cup shredded process American cheese
1 egg, beaten

1 cup finely chopped salted cashews
1 teaspoon dried parsley flakes
1 tablespoon butter or margarine

In a small bowl, combine rice, carrot, cheese and egg; mix well. Shape into 2 patties. In a shallow bowl, mix cashews and parsley flakes. Place patties in cashew mixture and turn to coat both sides. Melt butter or margarine in a medium skillet. Cook patties in butter or margarine until browned on one side. Turn and cook until browned on second side. Makes 2 servings.

Fresh Vegetable Stew

Use any type of summer squash—or try eggplant.

2 tablespoons vegetable oil
1 zucchini, cut in 1/4-inch slices
1/4 cup chopped green pepper
1/4 cup chopped onion

1 garlic clove, minced
1 (8-oz.) can whole tomatoes
2 tablespoons snipped fresh parsley
Dash hot pepper sauce

Heat oil in a medium skillet. Add zucchini, green pepper, onion and garlic. Cook and stir over medium-high heat until vegetables are tender. Add tomatoes, parsley and hot pepper sauce. Cook and stir until heated through. Makes 3 servings.

Fruited Sweet Potato Bake

Remember this pretty dish when you're planning your holiday menu.

2 tablespoons butter or margarine, melted
2 tablespoons orange juice
2 tablespoons brown sugar
1 (18-oz.) can vacuum-packed sweet
  potatoes, drained

Salt
1 (8-oz.) can jellied cranberry sauce,
  sliced
1 cup miniature marshmallows

Preheat oven to 375°F (190°C). In a 10" x 6" baking dish, combine butter or margarine, orange juice and brown sugar. Add sweet potatoes, turning to coat in mixture. Sprinkle lightly with salt. Cut cranberry sauce slices in half; arrange over sweet potatoes. Sprinkle with marshmallows. Bake about 20 minutes or until heated through and marshmallows are golden. Makes 4 servings.

Jiffy Soups & Sauces

Soups and sauces lend a special touch to any meal—and you don't need to spend all day over the hot stove making them! For example, to make a superb creamy vegetable soup, mix a package of frozen international vegetables, a can of cream soup such as mushroom, chicken, celery, onion or potato, plus a soup can or two of water for desired consistency. Simmer until the vegetables are tender, then serve from your favorite soup tureen.

Hot soup will stay hot longer if you first pour hot water into the tureen or soup bowls and let it stand a few minutes. Pour out the hot water, pour in the soup and serve it immediately.

Top soups with distinctive garnishes such as flavored croutons, shredded cheese, snipped parsley, chives or fresh herbs, crumbled crisp bacon or popcorn sprinkled with celery salt or onion salt. Even the most humble soup can be served proudly if it's topped with a dollop of sour cream or yogurt.

If you can't find a canned soup in your cupboard that appeals to you, why not combine two different soups to make a flavorful blend. It's also a useful trick when you're serving a crowd and your cupboard contains one can each of several different soups. Try these combinations:

- Bean with bacon soup plus minestrone soup and 2 soup cans of water.
- Beef broth plus tomato rice soup and 1-1/2 soup cans of water.
- Cream of chicken soup plus chicken gumbo soup and 2 soup cans of water.
- Chedder cheese soup plus tomato soup and 2 soup cans of water.
- Clam chowder plus vegetarian vegetable soup and 2 soup cans of water.

Enhance vegetables, chicken and fish with a smooth creamy sauce. To make a cream sauce in a hurry, heat condensed cream of mushroom, onion or celery soup with a little milk. Add a splash of white wine and a spoonful or two of shredded cheese. Sprinkle in a few seasonings such as pepper and two or three crushed dried herbs and your sauce is ready!

Give packaged sauce mixes a lift by adding a few extras such as herbs, snipped parsley or chives, drained canned mushrooms and a few tablespoons of wine or lemon juice. You can also stir in a little dry or prepared mustard, Worcestershire sauce, prepared horseradish or hot pepper sauce.

Sunshine Carrot Soup

Rice is the thickening agent for this soup.

2 tablespoons butter or margarine	1/4 teaspoon sugar
1/3 cup chopped onion	Dash pepper
2 tablespoons uncooked long-grain rice	Dash garlic salt
1 cup sliced frozen carrots	2 tablespoons orange juice
1 (14-1/2-oz.) can chicken broth	1/2 cup milk
2 parsley sprigs	Snipped fresh parsley or salad seasoning
1/4 teaspoon grated orange peel	

Melt butter or margarine in a medium saucepan. Add onion and rice. Stir over medium heat until onion is tender. Add carrots, chicken broth, parsley sprigs, orange peel, sugar, pepper and garlic salt. Cover and simmer gently until vegetables are very tender, about 20 minutes. Remove parsley sprig. Ladle soup into blender. Cover and process on high speed until smooth. Return soup to saucepan. Stir in orange juice, then milk. Reheat just until mixture comes to a boil. Serve in soup cups garnished with snipped parsley or salad seasoning. Makes 3 large or 6 small servings.

How to Make Sunshine Carrot Soup

1/Simmer frozen carrots, rice and orange peel in richly seasoned broth, then ladle into your blender.

2/Blend mixture until smooth, then reheat with milk and orange juice. Serve in soup cups. Garnish with parsley.

Sausage & Cheese Chowder

A can of potato soup gives you a head start on this sensational soup.

8 oz. bulk pork sausage
1/4 cup chopped celery
1/4 cup chopped onion
2 tablespoons chopped green pepper

1 (10-3/4-oz.) can condensed cream of
   potato soup
1 soup can milk
1 cup shredded Cheddar cheese (4 oz.)

In a medium saucepan, cook sausage, celery, onion and green pepper until vegetables are tender and meat is browned. Drain off excess fat. Blend in condensed soup and milk. Cook and stir over medium-high heat until mixture comes to a boil. Remove from heat; add cheese. Stir just until cheese melts. Serve at once. Makes 3 or 4 servings.

Sherried Crab Bisque

What could be more elegant than crab, mushrooms and sherry!

1 (14-1/2-oz.) can chicken broth
1 (10-3/4-oz.) can condensed tomato soup
1 (5-1/3-oz.) can evaporated milk
   (2/3 cup)
2 tablespoons dry sherry

1 (6-oz.) can crabmeat, drained, flaked
1 (2-1/2-oz.) jar sliced mushrooms,
   drained
Dash freshly ground pepper
Snipped fresh parsley

In a medium saucepan, combine chicken broth, condensed tomato soup, evaporated milk and sherry; mix well. Stir frequently over medium-high heat until mixture barely begins to boil but do not boil. Add crabmeat, mushrooms and pepper. Heat through. Garnish each serving with snipped parsley. Makes 4 servings.

Cheddar Clam Chowder

A quick soup with superb flavor.

1 (11-oz.) can condensed Cheddar
   cheese soup
1/2 cup milk
1 (8-oz.) can stewed tomatoes,
   cut up, undrained

1 (6-oz.) can minced clams, undrained
2 tablespoons dry white wine
Dash freshly ground pepper

In a medium saucepan, whisk cheese soup and milk until blended. Add stewed tomatoes, clams and wine. Season with pepper; mix well. Bring to a boil; remove from heat. Makes 4 servings.

Mexican Cheese Soup

If you're not a chili fan, use the cheese spread with pimiento.

1/2 cup finely chopped onion
1/2 cup shredded carrot
1/2 cup thinly sliced celery
1/3 cup butter or margarine
1/3 cup all-purpose flour
1 teaspoon paprika
1 teaspoon dry mustard
1 teaspoon Worcestershire sauce

1 (14-1/2-oz.) can chicken broth
1 cup milk
1/2 teaspoon liquid smoke
1 (8-oz.) jar pasteurized process cheese
   spread with jalapenos or pimiento
Canned chopped green chilies
Tortilla chips
Shredded Cheddar cheese

In a medium saucepan, cook onion, carrot, and celery in butter or margarine until tender. Stir in flour, paprika, dry mustard, and Worcestershire sauce until blended. Add chicken broth and milk. Stir over medium-high heat until mixture thickens and bubbles. Stir in liquid smoke. Reduce heat to very low. Add cheese spread to soup. Simmer 10 minutes, stirring occasionally. Place small pieces of chilies on tortilla chips; top with shredded cheese. Place on broiler pan. Broil 3 to 5 inches from heat at high temperature 1 to 1-1/2 minutes or until cheese melts. Ladle soup into bowls; top with tortilla chips. Makes 4 servings.

Bolshoi Beet Soup

Unusual and unusually good!

1 (16-oz.) can julienne-style beets
1 (14-1/2-oz.) can beef broth
1 (6-oz.) can tomato juice (3/4 cup)
2 tablespoons dried mixed vegetables for
  soups, stews and casseroles

2 teaspoons lemon juice
Dash garlic powder
Dairy sour cream

In a medium saucepan, combine undrained beets, beef broth, tomato juice, dried mixed vegetables, lemon juice and garlic powder. Bring to a boil; reduce heat. Cover and simmer 20 minutes or until mixed vegetables are tender. Top each serving with a dollop of sour cream; serve hot. Makes 3 servings.

Lazy-Day Bean Soup

Good old-fashioned flavor in 20 minutes!

1 (4-oz.) can Vienna sausages or
  3 frankfurters
1 (8-oz.) can baked beans
1/4 cup dried mixed vegetables for
  soups, stews and casseroles
1 (1-serving-size) envelope dried
  onion soup mix

2 cups water
1/4 teaspoon dried leaf thyme
Dash garlic powder
Dash pepper

Cut sausages or frankfurters into bite-size pieces. Combine all ingredients in a medium saucepan. Bring to a boil; reduce heat. Simmer uncovered 20 minutes. Makes 3 servings.

Horseradish-Mustard Sauce

The best thing that ever happened to leftover roast beef!

1/4 Horseradish-Mustard Sauce Stick,
  see below

1 cup water

Horseradish-Mustard Sauce Stick:
1/2 cup soft-style margarine
1 cup nonfat dry milk powder
1/2 cup non-dairy coffee creamer
1/2 cup all-purpose flour
2 vegetable bouillon cubes, crushed

1 tablespoon dry mustard
1 tablespoon prepared horseradish
1/2 teaspoon garlic salt
1/4 teaspoon pepper

Crumble piece of sauce stick into a saucepan. Add water. Whisk over medium-high heat until sauce thickens and bubbles. Serve over roast beef, ham or vegetables. Makes 1 cup of sauce.

Horseradish-Mustard Sauce Stick:
In a medium bowl, combine margarine, dry milk powder, coffee creamer, flour, crushed bouillon cubes, dry mustard, horseradish, garlic salt and pepper; mix well. Turn out onto a piece of waxed paper. Knead with your hands until mixture clings together. Shape into a stick. Use a table knife to score stick into quarters. Wrap in plastic wrap and refrigerate up to 2 to 3 weeks. Makes enough for 4 cups of sauce.

Garlic-Cheese Sauce

Delicious creamy cheese is the secret ingredient.

1/4 Garlic-Cheese Sauce Stick, see below
1 cup water

Garlic-Cheese Sauce Stick:
1 (4-oz.) carton semi-soft natural
   cheese with garlic and herbs
1/4 cup soft-style margarine
1 cup nonfat dry milk powder

1/2 cup non-dairy coffee creamer
1/2 cup all-purpose flour
1/4 cup instant chicken bouillon granules
1/4 teaspoon salt

Crumble piece of sauce stick into a saucepan. Add water. Whisk over medium-high heat until sauce thickens and bubbles. Serve over vegetables, chicken or fish. Makes about 1 cup of sauce.

Garlic-Cheese Sauce Stick:
In a small bowl, combine semi-soft cheese, margarine, dry milk powder, coffee creamer, flour, bouillon granules and salt; mix well. Turn out onto a piece of waxed paper. Knead with your hands until mixture clings together. Shape into a stick. Use a table knife to score stick in quarters. Wrap in plastic wrap and refrigerate up to 2 to 3 weeks. Makes enough for 4 cups of sauce.

How to Make Garlic Cheese Sauce

1/Semi-soft cheese is packaged in a small box. Knead cheese mixture, shape into a log and score in 4 equal pieces.

2/Combine 1/4 of the sauce stick and 1 cup water. Cook and stir until sauce thickens and bubbles. Pour over vegetables, chicken or fish.

Parmesan Sauce

With a sauce stick in your refrigerator, you're only a few minutes away from a flavorful sauce.

1/4 Parmesan Sauce Stick, see below
1 cup water

Parmesan Sauce Stick:

1/2 cup soft-style margarine
1 cup nonfat dry milk powder
1/2 cup non-dairy coffee creamer
1/2 cup all-purpose flour
1/2 cup grated Parmesan cheese

1 tablespoon dried parsley flakes
1 tablespoon dried chives
1/2 teaspoon salt
1/4 cup dry white wine

Crumble piece of sauce stick into a saucepan. Add water. Whisk over medium-high heat until sauce thickens and bubbles. Serve over vegetables, eggs or fish. Makes about 1 cup of sauce.

Parmesan Sauce Stick:
In a medium bowl, combine margarine, dry milk powder, coffee creamer, flour, Parmesan cheese, parsley flakes, dried chives and salt; mix well. Add wine; stir until blended. Turn out onto a piece of waxed paper. Knead with your hands until mixture clings together. Shape into a stick. Use a table knife to score stick into quarters. Wrap in plastic wrap and refrigerate up to 2 to 3 weeks. Makes enough for 4 cups of sauce.

Cheese-Mushroom Sauce

The finishing touch for a plain omelet.

1 tablespoon butter or margarine
1 (2-1/2-oz.) jar sliced mushrooms,
   drained
1 envelope cheese sauce mix

1/2 teaspoon dry mustard
1 teaspoon Worcestershire sauce
Milk

Melt butter or margarine in a small saucepan. Add mushrooms. Sauté 2 to 3 minutes over medium-high heat, stirring gently. Add cheese sauce mix, dry mustard and Worcestershire sauce. Add milk according to package directions. Stir over medium-high heat until sauce thickens and bubbles. Serve hot with vegetables or omelets. Makes 1-1/3 cups of sauce.

Herbed Sauce

Just-right seasoning to dress-up vegetables, chicken or fish.

1/4 Herbed Sauce Stick, see below
1 cup water

Herbed Sauce Stick:

1/2 cup soft-style margarine
1 cup nonfat dry milk powder
1/2 cup non-dairy coffee creamer
1/2 cup all-purpose flour
1/4 cup instant chicken bouillon granules

1 teaspoon fines herbes
1/2 teaspoon celery salt
1/4 teaspoon onion powder
1 tablespoon lemon juice

Crumble piece of sauce stick into a saucepan. Add water. Whisk over medium-high heat until sauce thickens and bubbles. Serve over vegetables, chicken or fish. Makes about 1 cup of sauce.

Herbed Sauce Stick:

In a medium bowl, combine margarine, dry milk powder, coffee creamer, flour, bouillon granules, fines herbes, celery salt, onion powder and lemon juice. Mix well. Turn out onto a piece of waxed paper. Knead with your hands until mixture clings together. Shape into a stick. Use a table knife to score stick into quarters. Wrap and refrigerate up to 2 to 3 weeks. Make enough for 4 cups of sauce.

Hollandaise Sauce Supreme

Increase the lemon flavor by adding 1 teaspoon lemon juice to the finished sauce.

1 envelope hollandaise sauce mix
1 teaspoon dried leaf tarragon, crushed
1 teaspoon snipped chives
1/2 teaspoon dried lemon peel

Water or other liquid
1/4 cup diced seeded peeled cucumber
1 tablespoon dry white wine

In a small saucepan, mix hollandaise sauce mix, tarragon, chives and lemon peel. Add water or other liquid called for on sauce mix envelope. Cook according to package directions. Stir in cucumber and wine. Heat through. Serve with fish or seafood. Makes about 1 cup of sauce.

Hurry Curry Sauce

Look for white sauce sticks in the refrigerated section of your grocery store.

1 tablespoon butter or margarine
3 tablespoons finely chopped green onion
1/2 to 1 teaspoon curry powder
1/4 teaspoon seasoned salt
1 teaspoon instant chicken
   bouillon granules

1 teaspoon lemon juice
Milk, water or vegetable liquid
   (for 1 cup sauce)
1/4 refrigerated white sauce stick
   (for 1 cup sauce)

Melt butter or margarine in a small saucepan. Add onion and curry powder. Cook until onion is tender but not browned. Add seasoned salt, chicken bouillon granules, lemon juice and milk, water or vegetable liquid called for in package directions to make 1 cup of white sauce. Bring to a boil. Slice piece of sauce stick into mixture. Whisk over medium-high heat until sauce thickens and boils. Serve over poached eggs, green vegetables or rice. Makes 1 cup of sauce.

Variations

Chicken Curry: Add 1 cup diced cooked chicken and 1/2 cup drained canned pineapple chunks. Heat through. Serve over hot cooked rice. Sprinkle with minced parsley. Serve with curry condiments such as almonds, chutney, and diced cucumber mixed with yogurt.

Pork Curry: Add 1 cup diced cooked pork and 1/2 cup finely chopped peeled apple. Heat through. Serve over hot cooked rice. Sprinkle with minced parsley. Serve with curry condiments such as raisins, peanuts and shredded coconut.

Shortcut Breads

Alternatives to freshly baked breads are convenience breads from the supermarket freezer, packaged mixes, or bakery specialties. You can give them your own homemade touch with herb butters, spices and a bit of cheese. For example:

• Brush brown-and-serve rolls with melted butter, then sprinkle them with sesame seeds, poppy seeds or a mixture of herbs. Bake the rolls according to package directions and serve hot.
• Melt butter in a baking dish. Coat refrigerated biscuits in the butter and sprinkle them with crumbled blue cheese or grated Parmesan cheese. Bake them according to package directions. Cheese-flavored biscuits are marvelous with soups and stews.
• Cut a loaf of thawed frozen whole-wheat bread dough into 8 pieces. Shape the pieces into rolls then brush them with butter and sprinkle with chopped nuts. Bake the rolls according to package directions and serve them with honey butter.
• Use packaged biscuit mix to make drop biscuits—there's no kneading, rolling or cutting! Serve hot biscuits with jam.
• Prepare corn muffin mix according to package directions. Before baking, fold 1/2 cup of drained canned corn and 1/2 cup of shredded Swiss cheese into the batter. Bake according to package directions.
• Brush refrigerated crescent roll dough triangles with butter. Sprinkle with cinnamon, sugar and raisins. Roll up the triangles and bake according to package directions. Spicy crescents are also delicious for brunch or with morning coffee.
• Bake blueberry muffin mix according to package directions. Dip the tops of the warm muffins in melted butter, then in a mixture of sugar, ground cinnamon and grated lemon peel. Serve them with a late supper of omelets or scrambled eggs.

Making your own croutons to sprinkle on salads or soups is easier than you think. It's also a thrifty way to make use of bread you haven't had a chance to use. Preheat your oven to 250°F (120°C). Remove crusts and spread the bread lightly with butter. Cut the bread into 1/2-inch cubes. Spread the cubes in a single layer in a shallow baking pan. Bake them in the preheated oven until they are crisp and golden, stirring and turning occasionally with a spatula.

Toasted Cheese Slices

Toast sesame seeds in a 300°F (150°C) oven for 15 to 20 minutes, turning frequently.

1/2 (5-oz.) jar sharp process cheese
  spread with bacon
4 tablespoons butter or margarine,
  softened
1/2 teaspoon dry mustard

3 tablespoons butter or margarine,
  softened
8 or 9 French bread slices
Poppy seeds or toasted sesame seeds

In a small bowl, combine cheese spread, 4 tablespoons butter or margarine and dry mustard. Beat with electric mixer on high speed until fluffy. On a preheated griddle or in a large skillet, melt 3 tablespoons butter or margarine. Place bread on griddle or in skillet. Cook until browned on one side. Turn bread. Spread browned side with cheese mixture and sprinkle with poppy seeds or sesame seeds. Cook until other side is browned. Makes 8 or 9 slices.

Cream Cheese & Garlic Bread

Early in the day, set out the cream cheese and butter or margarine to soften.

1 (3-oz.) pkg. cream cheese, softened
2 tablespoons butter or margarine,
  softened

1/4 teaspoon garlic powder
3 tablespoons butter or margarine
2 slices French bread, cut 1 inch thick

In a small bowl, combine cream cheese, 2 tablespoons butter or margarine and garlic powder. Beat with electric mixer on high speed until smooth. On a preheated griddle or in a large skillet, melt 3 tablespoons butter or margarine. Add bread. Cook until browned on one side. Turn bread. Spread browned side with about 2 tablespoons cream cheese mixture. Cook until other side is browned. Serve warm. Store remaining cream cheese mixture in refrigerator for another use. Makes 2 servings.

Garlic Breadsticks

Try these with Wilted Spinach Salad, page 90.

2 tablespoons butter or margarine, melted
1/2 teaspoon garlic salt
1 (3.75-oz.) tube refrigerated biscuits
  (6 biscuits)

2 tablespoons sesame seeds or poppy seeds

Preheat oven to 450°F (230°C). In a pie plate, combine melted butter or margarine and garlic salt. On a lightly floured surface, use your hands to roll each biscuit into a thin stick about 8 inches long. Roll sticks in melted garlic butter. Place on waxed paper. Sprinkle sticks on all sides with sesame seeds or poppy seeds. Bake on ungreased baking sheet 8 to 10 minutes or until lightly browned. Makes 6 breadsticks.

Herb-Seasoned Croutons

Great for soups or salads—or just for munching.

2 slices white bread
6 tablespoons butter or margarine

1 tablespoon dried minced onion flakes
1 teaspoon dried leaf marjoram

Cut bread in 1/2-inch cubes. Melt butter or margarine in a medium skillet. Stir in onion flakes and marjoram. Add bread cubes. Cook and stir over medium-high heat until toasted. Makes 3/4 cup of croutons.

Cinnamon-Honey Waffles

You'll like the delicious syrup on pancakes and French toast, too.

2 tablespoons butter or margarine
4 frozen waffles, thawed
1/2 cup honey

4 tablespoons butter or margarine
1/4 cup raisins
1 teaspoon ground cinnamon

Heat 2 tablespoons butter or margarine in a large skillet. Cook waffles until browned. Turn and cook until other side is browned. In a small saucepan, combine honey, 4 tablespoons butter or margarine, raisins and cinnamon. Cook and stir until butter or margarine is melted and syrup is warm. Serve over waffles. Makes 2 servings.

Mama's Chocolate Toast

A delicious variation of cinnamon toast!

3 tablespoons sugar
1 teaspoon unsweetened cocoa powder

Butter or margarine, softened
2 slices bread

Mix sugar and cocoa in a small bowl. Spread butter or margarine on both sides of bread. Sprinkle both sides with sugar mixture; shake off excess. Cook on preheated griddle until browned on one side. Turn bread. Sprinkle browned side with 1/2 teaspoon sugar mixture. Brown other side. Remove from griddle. Sprinkle with remaining sugar mixture. Makes 2 servings.

Cheese-Herb Bread

Grilled French bread sprinkled with herb-flavored cheese is almost like home-baked.

3 tablespoons butter or margarine
2 slices French bread, cut 1 inch thick
2 tablespoons grated Parmesan cheese

1/4 teaspoon dried rosemary
1/4 teaspoon dried leaf thyme

Melt butter or margarine on preheated griddle or in skillet. Add bread and cook until browned on one side. In a small bowl or cup, mix Parmesan cheese, rosemary and thyme. Turn bread and sprinkle browned side with cheese mixture. Cook until other side is browned. Makes 2 servings.

Coffeetime Cutouts

Decorating these sweet and savory treats is almost as much fun as eating them.

1 (8-oz.) tube refrigerated crescent rolls
About 2 tablespoons butter or margarine, melted
1 tablespoon sugar
1/4 teaspoon ground allspice

Red or green powdered gelatin
Mixed dried leaf herbs such as dillweed, oregano and basil
Seasoned salts such as celery salt and onion salt

Preheat oven to 375°F (190°C). Grease a baking sheet. Unroll crescent roll dough on a lightly floured surface. Pinch together perforations in the dough. Use small floured cookie cutters to cut out desired shapes. Brush with melted butter. In a small bowl, combine sugar and allspice. Sprinkle on a third of the cutouts. Sprinkle another third of the cutouts with dry gelatin. Combine herbs and seasoned salts in a small bowl. Sprinkle herb mixture over remaining cutouts. Bake on greased baking sheet 10 to 11 minutes. Makes 15 to 18 cutouts.

How to Make Coffeetime Cutouts

1/Cut shapes from crescent roll dough. Brush with melted butter or margarine; sprinkle with desired flavoring.

2/Bake cutouts 10 to 11 minutes. Serve warm with mugs of piping hot coffee or cocoa.

Sticky Buns Tropicale

Let the dough thaw overnight in your refrigerator.

1 (14-oz.) loaf frozen sweet roll
   dough or 1 (16-oz.) loaf frozen white
   bread dough, thawed
1 (3-1/8-oz.) pkg. regular coconut
   cream pudding mix

1/2 cup packed brown sugar
1/2 cup chopped macadamia nuts or pecans
1 teaspoon ground cinnamon
5 tablespoons butter or margarine, melted

Preheat oven to 350°F (175°C). Grease 16 muffin pan cups. Quarter loaf; cut each quarter into 8 cubes to make 32 cubes in all. In a medium bowl, mix dry pudding mix, brown sugar, nuts and cinnamon. Dip each dough cube in melted butter or margarine, then roll generously in pudding mixture. Place 2 coated balls in each muffin cup. Drizzle with any remaining butter and sprinkle with any remaining pudding mixture. Cover and let rise in a warm place until almost doubled in bulk, about 1 hour. Bake 12 minutes or until browned and buns have slightly pulled away from sides of cups. Let stand 2 minutes. Invert buns onto a rack to cool. Makes 16 buns.

How to Make Sticky Buns Tropicale

1/Cut bread dough into cubes. Dip into melted butter or margarine, then in dry pudding mixture. Place 2 cubes in each muffin cup.

2/Let baked buns stand in muffin cups 2 minutes before inverting them onto a wire rack to cool slightly. Serve warm with lots of whipped butter or margarine.

Sesame Cheese Bread

To toast sesame seeds, see Toasted Cheese Slices, page 115.

3-3/4 cups biscuit mix
1-1/2 cups shredded sharp process
  American cheese (6 oz.)

1 tablespoon toasted sesame seeds
1 egg, slightly beaten
1-1/2 cups beer or milk

Preheat oven to 350°F (175°C). Grease a 9" x 5" loaf pan. In a large bowl, stir biscuit mix, cheese and sesame seeds. Add egg and beer or milk. Mix to just moisten biscuit mix. Beat vigorously by hand 1 minute. Turn batter into greased loaf pan. Bake 1 hour or until golden brown. Cool in pan 10 minutes. Remove from pan and place on a rack. Makes 1 loaf.

Posh Pan Rolls

A quick dress-up for tea rolls from the bakery.

12 small baked pan rolls (8-inch pan)
1 cup powdered sugar
2 tablespoons thawed frozen orange
  juice concentrate

1 tablespoon hot water
1 to 2 teaspoons grated orange peel

Preheat oven to 375°F (190°C). Cover rolls loosely with foil. Heat in oven 10 minutes or until hot. In a small bowl, combine powdered sugar, orange juice concentrate and hot water; mix well. Dip each hot roll into orange glaze; place on serving plate. Sprinkle with grated orange peel. Serve at once. Makes 12 rolls.

Parmesan Shortcake Wedges

Perfect with soup or salad. The flavor is fabulous!

2 cups biscuit mix
Milk
1/2 cup chopped onion
1/2 cup grated Parmesan cheese

1/2 cup mayonnaise or mayonnaise-style
  salad dressing
1/4 teaspoon fines herbes

Preheat oven to 400°F (205°C). Grease a 12-inch pizza pan. Prepare biscuit dough with milk according to package directions for Rolled Biscuits. On a lightly floured surface, roll out dough to a 10-inch circle. Place in greased pizza pan, turning edges up slightly. Mix onion, Parmesan cheese, and mayonnaise or salad dressing; spread evenly over dough. Sprinkle with fines herbes. Bake 15 to 20 minutes or until browned. Cut in wedges and serve at once. Makes 8 servings.

Italian Dinner Wedges

It's a little different from the bread traditionally served with spaghetti and lasagna.

1 (10- to 12-inch) ready-to-bake
  pizza crust
2 tablespoons butter or margarine, melted
1/2 teaspoon instant minced onion

1 cup shredded Monterey Jack cheese
  (4 oz.)
Salad seasoning

Preheat oven to 450°F (230°C). Place pizza crust on a 12-inch pizza pan. Brush with melted butter or margarine. Sprinkle with instant minced onion, then shredded cheese. Sprinkle liberally with salad seasoning. Bake on bottom rack of oven 13 to 15 minutes. Cut in wedges and serve at once. Makes 8 to 12 wedges.

Jiffy Parmesan Bread

Press butter-coated refrigerated rolls into a loaf shape for a quick tasty bread.

3 tablespoons butter or margarine
1 (8-oz.) tube refrigerated flaky-type
  rolls (12 rolls)

Sesame seeds
Grated parmesan cheese

Preheat oven to 375°F (190°C). Melt butter or margarine in a 9'' x 5'' loaf pan. Separate each flaky roll into 2 pieces. Dip each piece in melted butter or margarine, then sprinkle with sesame seeds and Parmesan cheese. Shape into a loaf in baking pan. Sprinkle top of loaf with more sesame seeds and Parmesan cheese. Bake 12 to 14 minutes or until browned. Makes 1 loaf.

Taco Bread Bites

Easy and simply delicious! Chili fans will want to use the whole can of chilies.

2/3 cup finely chopped onion
1/3 cup butter or margarine
1/2 to 1 (4-oz.) can chopped green chilies

1 (16-oz.) loaf frozen bread dough, thawed
1/2 envelope taco seasoning
  (2 tablespoons)

Preheat oven to 400°F (205°C). Grease a 15'' x 10'' jelly-roll pan. In a medium skillet, sauté onion in butter or margarine until tender. Pat chilies dry on paper towels. Add chilies to sautéed onions; set aside. Pat bread dough evenly into greased jelly-roll pan. Sprinkle with taco seasoning, then spread with onion mixture. Cover and let rise in a warm place about 30 minutes or until almost doubled in bulk. Bake 22 to 24 minutes or until browned. Use kitchen shears to snip bread into serving-size pieces; serve hot. Makes 6 to 8 servings.

Skip-a-Step Desserts

Ice cream is a versatile, quick and easy dessert. Keep two or three different kinds in your freezer and you'll have the base for a variety of scrumptious desserts.

There is a secret to perfect whipped cream: be sure the cream, beaters and bowl are thoroughly chilled. Cream that has been refrigerated for a day or two whips easier than chilled fresh cream. Whip the cream until it mounds and holds its shape, but do not overbeat it. If you add sugar, fold it in after the cream is beaten. You can count on about 2 cups of whipped cream from 1 cup of cream. Use whipped cream promptly or chill it briefly before using.

Now that you're prepared with ice cream in your freezer and and you know the secret of perfect whipped cream, here are some ideas to add quick variety to your dessert selection:

● Spread coffee ice cream in a graham cracker pie crust or chocolate-wafer pie crust. Then spread the ice cream with thick fudge ice cream topping and sprinkle with chopped nuts or coconut. Store your delicious ice cream pie in the freezer or serve it immediately.

● You can do wonders with a little liqueur, frozen fruit and sherbet. Stir a few tablespoons of creme de cassis into thawed frozen sweetened raspberries and spoon the sauce over raspberry sherbet. Or stir a few tablespoons of Cherry Heering into thawed frozen sweetened cherries and serve over lemon sherbet.

● Top slices of bakery angel food cake or thawed frozen pound cake with fresh or thawed frozen fruit and whipped cream or whipped topping. Or top cake with a scoop of ice cream, sliced bananas and your favorite ice cream sauce.

● Bake frozen patty shells. Fill them with ice cream or canned or instant pudding mixed with chopped nuts and coconut.

● Make an inside-out shortcake. Frost sponge cake shortcake cups with whipped cream or whipped topping and fill with berries or sliced fresh fruit.

● Bake refrigerated slice-and-bake cookies. Sandwich the cookies together with canned frosting, or spread frosting on the cookies and sprinkle with chopped candy. Spread peanut butter cookies with peanut butter and sprinkle with chopped peanuts.

● Prepare packaged gingerbread mix and bake according to package directions. Fold applesauce and ground cinnamon into whipped topping and serve it over warm gingerbread squares.

Fruit Kabobs au Natural

Get out your skewers for this quick summertime treat.

1 small peach, cut in 1-inch cubes
1 small apple, cut in 1-inch cubes
1 small banana, cut in 1-inch sections
3/4 cup fresh pineapple, cut in
  1-inch cubes

3/4 cup fresh strawberries
1/4 cup honey
1 tablespoon lemon juice
4 tablespoons butter or margarine

Thread fruits alternately on 6 skewers. In a small bowl or cup, mix honey and lemon juice. On preheated griddle, melt butter or margarine. Place kabobs on griddle. Cook over medium-high heat until heated through, turning and brushing frequently with honey mixture. Makes 6 kabobs.

Apple Brown Betty

Keep brown sugar soft by storing it with a piece of bread in a tightly covered container.

1 (3.75-oz.) tube refrigerated biscuits
  (6 biscuits)
1/2 cup packed brown sugar
1 tablespoon ground cinnamon
6 tablespoons butter or margarine
2 medium apples, peeled, cored,
  thinly sliced

1 tablespoon cornstarch
1 tablespoon brown sugar
1/2 teaspoon ground cinnamon
1 cup apple juice
1 teaspoon lemon juice
Ice cream or whipped topping

On a lightly floured surface, roll each biscuit into a 3-1/2-inch circle. In a pie plate, mix 1/2 cup brown sugar and 1 tablespoon cinnamon. Coat both sides of biscuits with sugar-cinnamon mixture. Melt 1-1/2 tablespoons butter or margarine on a preheated griddle. Place 3 biscuits at a time on griddle. Cook until browned, about 1 minute on each side. Remove biscuits and keep warm. Repeat with remaining biscuits and 1-1/2 tablespoons butter or margarine. Melt remaining 3 tablespoons butter or margarine in a medium skillet. Add apple slices. Cook and stir over medium-high heat until tender, about 8 minutes. Keep warm. In a medium saucepan, mix cornstarch, 1 tablespoon brown sugar and 1/2 teaspoon cinnamon. Stir in apple juice. Cook and stir until mixture is thickened and bubbly. Add lemon juice. Stir in apple slices. In 3 dessert bowls, make 1 layer each of apple mixture, grilled biscuit and ice cream or whipped topping. Serve with additional grilled cinnamon biscuits. Makes 3 servings.

Cranberry Crunch Parfaits

After a meal of leftover turkey, this is the perfect dessert.

2 tablespoons butter or margarine
1/4 cup quick-cooking oats
2 tablespoons brown sugar
2 tablespoons chopped pecans
1/4 teaspoon ground cinnamon

1/2 cup granulated sugar
1/2 cup water
1 cup fresh cranberries
Vanilla ice cream

Melt butter or margarine in a small skillet. Add oats, brown sugar, pecans and cinnamon. Cook and stir over medium-high heat until brown and crumbly. Remove from heat and set aside. In a small saucepan, combine granulated sugar and water; stir until dissolved. Add cranberries. Cook until most of the skins have popped, about 5 minutes; cool. In 2 or 3 parfait glasses, layer ice cream, cooked cranberries and oat mixture. Makes 2 or 3 servings.

How to Make Cranberry Crunch Parfaits

Layer ice cream, cranberries and crumb topping in parfait glasses or water goblets. Repeat layers, ending with crumb topping.

Picture-Pretty Parfaits

- Make a tropical treat with layers of pineapple sherbet, toasted coconut, macadamia nuts and crushed pineapple in parfait glasses or water goblets.
- Swirl peanut butter into vanilla ice cream. In parfait glasses, layer the ice cream mixture with chopped salted peanuts and butterscotch sauce.
- Stir ground cinnamon and nutmeg into vanilla ice cream. Break up pieces of leftover apple pie in chunks. Layer apple pie chunks, spiced ice cream and shredded Cheddar cheese in parfait glasses or a pretty glass bowl.
- Mix canned cherry pie filling with a few tablespoons of cherry brandy, then layer the brandied pie filling with canned vanilla pudding.

Tropic Isle Banana Splits

Ignite this flaming extravaganza at the table in a chafing dish.

4 tablespoons butter or margarine
1/4 cup shredded coconut
1/4 cup packed brown sugar
1/2 teaspoon ground cinnamon
1 cup fresh peach slices or 1 (8-3/4-oz.) can peach slices, drained

1/4 cup heated rum
2 small bananas, split lengthwise
Vanilla, chocolate and strawberry ice cream
Maraschino cherries, if desired

Melt butter or margarine in a small skillet. Add coconut. Cook and stir over medium-high heat until toasted. Remove coconut and set aside; reserve butter or margarine in skillet. Stir in brown sugar and cinnamon. Add peaches. Cook and stir until heated through. Ignite heated rum and pour over peaches. Cook and stir until flame subsides. Line 2 banana split dishes with banana halves. Top with scoops of vanilla, chocolate and strawberry ice cream. Spoon peach mixture over ice cream and sprinkle with toasted coconut. Top with maraschino cherries, if desired. Makes 2 servings.

Chocolate-Mint Ice Cream Bars

Use your favorite ice cream to vary the flavor of this crunchy bar.

4 tablespoons butter or margarine
2 cups crushed cream-filled chocolate cookies (about 16)
1 qt. mint chocolate chip ice cream, softened

4 tablespoons butter or margarine
1/2 cup flaked coconut
1/2 cup chopped pecans

Melt 4 tablespoons butter or margarine in a small skillet. In a 9" x 5" baking dish, mix melted butter or margarine and 1-3/4 cups of the cookie crumbs. Pat into bottom of baking dish to make a crust. Spread softened ice cream on crust and place in freezer. In the same skillet, melt 4 tablespoons butter or margarine. Stir in coconut and pecans. Cook and stir until coconut is lightly toasted. Stir in remaining 1/4 cup cookie crumbs; cool. Sprinkle cooled pecan mixture on top of ice cream. Freeze 2 hours or longer. Remove from freezer 15 minutes before serving. Cut into squares. Makes 8 servings.

Double-Fudge Sundaes

Put off making this until your figure can afford it.

1 (5-1/3-oz.) can evaporated milk
  (2/3 cup)
1 (6-oz.) pkg. chocolate chips (1 cup)
1/2 (1-pt.) jar marshmallow creme

Chocolate ice cream
Whipped topping
Chopped nuts
Maraschino cherries, if desired

Combine milk and chocolate chips in a medium saucepan. Cook and stir over low heat until chocolate chips just melt. Stir in marshmallow creme. Beat until melted. Pour over chocolate ice cream. Spoon whipped topping and nuts over sauce. Top with maraschino cherries, if desired. Makes 4 to 6 servings.

Berry Peach Crisp

Pack brown sugar into a measuring cup, then level the sugar by pressing with the heel of your hand.

4 tablespoons butter or margarine
1 cup quick-cooking oats
1/4 cup packed brown sugar
1 cup blueberry pie filling

1 (8-3/4-oz.) can peach slices, drained
1 tablespoon lemon juice
Whipped topping

Melt butter or margarine in a small skillet. Add oats and brown sugar. Cook and stir until heated through. Divide mixture among 4 dessert bowls; reserve 1/4 cup for topping. In a small saucepan, combine blueberry pie filling, peach slices and lemon juice. Cook and stir gently until peach mixture is heated through. Spoon over oat mixture. Top with whipped topping and reserved oat mixture. Makes 4 servings.

Fruit Compote Bake

What a warm and wonderful way to end a brunch!

1 (8-oz.) can pineapple slices
1 orange, thinly sliced
1 cup dried pitted prunes
1/4 cup packed brown sugar
1/4 cup cream sherry or orange juice

2 teaspoons quick-cooking tapioca
1/2 teaspoon shredded orange peel
1/2 teaspoon ground cinnamon
1/4 teaspoon ground nutmeg

Preheat oven to 350°F (175°C). Drain pineapple slices; reserve 1/4 cup liquid. Cut pineapple and orange slices in half. Arrange pineapple slices, orange slices and prunes in a 1-quart casserole. In a small bowl, combine brown sugar, cream sherry or orange juice, reserved pineapple syrup, tapioca, orange peel, cinnamon and nutmeg. Pour mixture over fruit in casserole. Mix gently to distribute tapioca. Bake 35 minutes, stirring once about halfway through baking time. Cool until warm. Spoon into sherbet dishes. Makes 4 servings.

1-2-3 Lime Pie

The crisp crust is filled with light-as-a-cloud filling.

1 (6-oz.) can frozen limeade
   concentrate, thawed
1 (14-oz.) can sweetened condensed milk
Few drops green food coloring
1 (8-oz.) carton frozen whipped dessert
   topping, thawed

1 (9-inch) graham cracker or
   chocolate cookie pie crust
Whipped dessert topping
Chocolate curls or lime slices

Mix limeade concentrate and sweetened condensed milk in a medium bowl. Whisk just until blended. Whisk in food coloring; mix well. Fold in dessert topping. Turn mixture into pie crust. Refrigerate until firm, about 3 hours. To serve, garnish with additional whipped topping and chocolate curls or lime slices. Makes 6 servings.

How to Make 1-2-3 Lime Pie

1/Whisk together limeade concentrate and condensed milk until smooth. Fold in whipped topping. Spoon into chocolate or graham cracker crust; chill.

2/Use a vegetable peeler to shave chocolate curls from a chocolate bar. Pick curls up with a wooden pick to prevent breaking. Gently place curls on pie.

Chocolate Velvet Pie

Be sure to use a presweetened cocoa powder for the topping.

1 (4-1/4- or 4-1/2-oz.) pkg. instant
  chocolate pudding mix
1 pt. chocolate ice cream, softened
1/2 cup milk

2 tablespoons creme de cacao
1 (9-inch) graham cracker pie crust
Cocoa Whipped Topping, see below

Cocoa Whipped Topping:
1 envelope dessert topping mix
1/2 cup cold milk

1/2 teaspoon vanilla extract
1/4 cup presweetened cocoa powder

In a small bowl, combine instant pudding mix, ice cream, milk, and creme de cacao. Beat with electric mixer on low speed until blended, about 2 minutes. Pour into crust. Refrigerate while making topping. Prepare Cocoa Whipped Topping. Spread topping over pie. Freeze until firm. Makes 6 servings.

Cocoa Whipped Topping:
In a deep bowl, mix dessert topping mix, cold milk, vanilla and cocoa powder. Beat with electric mixer on high speed until peaks form. Continue beating until smooth and fluffy, about 2 minutes.

Peach Melba Pudding

Impress someone special with this elegant dessert.

1 (10-oz.) pkg. frozen sweetened
  raspberries, thawed
2 tablespoons cornstarch

1 tablespoon Cherry Heering liqueur
2 canned or fresh peach halves
2 (5-oz.) cans vanilla pudding

Drain raspberries; reserve syrup. Combine cornstarch and reserved raspberry syrup in a small saucepan. Cook and stir until thickened and bubbly. Stir in raspberries and Cherry Heering liqueur. Cook and stir gently until heated through; cool. In 2 sherbet glasses, layer peach halves, some of the raspberry sauce and pudding. Top with remaining raspberry sauce. Makes 2 servings.

Summertime Strawberry Tarts

Enjoy these tarts all year—use frozen strawberries for Wintertime Strawberry Tarts.

1-1/4 cups fresh or thawed frozen
   strawberries (not in syrup)
2 dessert tart shells
1/4 cup water

2 tablespoons sugar
2 teaspoons cornstarch
Whipped topping

Halve strawberries. Place 1/2 cup strawberries in each tart shell. In a small saucepan, crush remaining 1/4 cup strawberries; add water. Cook until strawberries are softened, about 1 minute. Press through a sieve. In the same saucepan, mix sugar and cornstarch; gradually stir sieved strawberry juice into sugar-cornstarch mixture. Cook and stir until thickened and bubbly. Pour syrup over strawberries in tart shells; refrigerate. Top with whipped topping before serving. Makes 2 servings.

Sunny Lemon Tarts

Pucker up!

3/4 cup sugar
3 tablespoons cornstarch
1 cup hot water
2 egg yolks
1 tablespoon butter or margarine

1 teaspoon grated lemon peel
1/4 cup lemon juice
4 dessert tart shells
Whipped topping

Combine sugar and cornstarch in a small saucepan. Gradually stir in hot water. Cook and stir until thickened and bubbly. Spoon about 1/4 cup mixture into egg yolks; mix well. Add egg yolk mixture to cornstarch mixture. Add butter or margarine and lemon peel. Stir until butter or margarine is melted. Add lemon juice. Beat until smooth. Spoon into tart shells; chill. Top with whipped topping. Makes 4 servings.

Praline Sundaes

Smooth butterscotch-pecan sauce is too good to resist.

1 egg yolk, slightly beaten
1/3 cup packed brown sugar
3 tablespoons light corn syrup
2 tablespoons chopped pecans

2 tablespoons water
2 tablespoons butter or margarine
Vanilla ice cream

In a small saucepan, combine all ingredients except ice cream. Cook and stir over medium heat until mixture thickens and boils. Serve over ice cream. Makes 1/2 cup of sauce.

Cinnamon-Apple Turnovers

Fruit-filled turnovers will disappear as soon as you take them out of the oven.

1 tablespoon all-purpose flour
1 tablespoon sugar
Dash ground cinnamon
Dash ground nutmeg
1/2 cup chopped peeled apple
2 tablespoons shredded Cheddar cheese

1 tablespoon raisins
1 stick pie crust mix
Water
2 tablespoons sugar
1/2 teaspoon ground cinnamon

Preheat oven to 425°F (220°C). In a medium bowl, mix flour, 1 tablespoon sugar, dash of cinnamon and nutmeg. Toss with apple, cheese and raisins; set aside. Prepare pie crust with water according to package directions. Roll out dough to a 12-inch square. Cut into nine 4-inch squares. Spoon apple filling on half of each square. Fold other half over filling to form a triangle. Moisten edges of pastry and seal with tines of a fork. In a small bowl or cup, mix 2 tablespoons sugar and 1/2 teaspoon cinnamon. Sprinkle over turnovers. Place on a baking sheet. Bake 12 to 13 minutes or until golden brown. Makes 9 turnovers.

How to Make Cinnamon-Apple Turnovers

1/Spoon the raisin and apple filling onto one side of each pastry square.

2/Moisten edges of pastry with water, then fold over and seal with tines of a fork.

Spiced Peach Dumplings

If you pit the peaches before wrapping them in dough, the dumplings will have an irregular shape.

1 (29-oz.) jar spiced peaches (6 peaches)
2 tablespoons cornstarch
1/3 cup peach brandy

2 sticks pie crust mix
Water
Cream

Preheat oven to 425°F (220°C). Drain peaches; reserve syrup. If necessary add water to syrup to measure 1-1/2 cups. Pat peaches dry with paper towels. Place cornstarch in a small saucepan. Slowly blend in reserved peach syrup. Stir constantly over medium-high heat until mixture thickens and bubbles. Stir in brandy; set aside. Prepare pastry sticks with water according to package directions. On a lightly floured board, roll out dough to a 16-1/2" x 11" rectangle. With a pastry wheel, cut into six 5-1/2-inch squares. Place a peach in the center of each square. Bring corners of dough together and pinch to seal. Place dumplings in a 12" x 7" baking dish. Pour syrup over dumplings. Bake 40 minutes or until golden brown. Spoon dumplings into dessert dishes and drizzle with syrup. Serve with cream. Makes 6 servings.

Blueberry & Cream Cheese Pie

If the pie is thoroughly chilled, it will cut easier.

1 (8-oz.) pkg. cream cheese, softened
1 (14-oz.) can sweetened condensed milk
1/2 cup lemon juice
1 teaspoon vanilla extract
1 (9-inch) graham cracker pie crust

3/4 cup sugar
2 tablespoons cornstarch
2 cups fresh or thawed frozen blueberries
1/2 cup water

In a medium bowl, beat cream cheese with mixer on high speed until light and fluffy. With mixer on medium speed, gradually beat in condensed milk. Beat until blended. Stir in lemon juice and vanilla. Pour into pie crust. Refrigerate 2 to 3 hours. In a small saucepan, combine sugar and cornstarch. Crush 1/2 cup blueberries; reserve remaining blueberries. Add crushed blueberries and water to sugar mixture. Cook and stir until thickened and bubbly; cool. Arrange whole blueberries on pie. Pour glaze over pie. Chill before serving. Makes one 9-inch pie.

Spicy Pear Crisp

Melted cheese is the secret ingredient that makes this dessert special.

1 (29-oz.) can pear slices
1/2 cup shredded process American cheese
1/2 pkg. 2-layer spice cake mix with
  pudding (about 2 cups)

1/4 cup quick-cooking oats
1/4 cup packed brown sugar
1/3 cup butter or margarine
Vanilla ice cream

Preheat oven to 350°F (175°C). Drain pears; reserve 1/3 cup syrup. Cut up pears and place in the bottom of a 10" x 6" baking dish. Pour reserved syrup over pears. Sprinkle with cheese, then cake mix, oats and brown sugar. Cut butter or margarine into small pieces and dot evenly over brown sugar. Bake 50 to 55 minutes. Serve warm. Top with vanilla ice cream. Makes 6 servings.

Blueberry-Walnut Torte

Take advantage of packaged mixes and combine them with nuts, fruit and yogurt.

1 (13.5-oz.) pkg. blueberry muffin mix
1 egg
Milk or water

1 cup finely chopped walnuts
Lemon Filling, see below
1 cup fresh or thawed frozen blueberries

Lemon Filling:
1 (3-3/4-oz.) pkg. instant lemon
   pudding mix

1 cup milk
1 (8-oz.) carton lemon yogurt

Preheat oven to 350°F (175°C). Grease and flour two 8-inch, round pans. Prepare blueberry muffin mix with egg and milk or water according to package directions. Stir walnuts into batter. Pour batter into prepared pans. Bake 25 minutes or until a wooden pick inserted in center comes out clean. Cool in pans 10 minutes. Invert to remove from pans. Cool on racks. Prepare Lemon Filling. Place one cooled cake layer on a platter. Spread half the Lemon Filling over the cake and sprinkle with half the blueberries. Place second layer on blueberries. Spread with remaining Lemon Filling and sprinkle with remaining blueberries. Makes 8 servings.

Lemon Filling:
In a small bowl, beat pudding mix and milk with mixer on low speed 2 minutes. Stir in yogurt.

Mocha Wacky Cake

Mix-in-the-pan cakes are not only easy—but fun!

1-1/2 cups all-purpose flour
1 cup packed brown sugar
1/4 cup unsweetened cocoa powder
1 teaspoon baking soda
1/2 teaspoon salt

1 tablespoon lemon juice
1/3 cup vegetable oil
1 teaspoon vanilla extract
1 cup cold strong coffee
Coffee ice cream

Preheat oven to 350°F (175°C). In an 8-inch square baking pan, stir together flour, brown sugar, cocoa powder, baking soda and salt. Make a well in center of mixture. Add lemon juice, oil and vanilla to well. Stir with a fork until all dry ingredients are moistened. Add coffee. Stir until batter is smooth and thoroughly mixed. Bake 25 to 30 minutes or until a wooden pick inserted in center comes out clean. Serve warm with scoops of coffee ice cream. Makes 9 to 12 servings.

Easy Ambrosia Cobbler

For a crowd, use all the cake mix, double the other ingredients and bake in 2 baking dishes.

1 (8-1/4-oz.) can crushed pineapple,
  undrained
1/2 (21-oz.) can apricot pie filling
  (1 cup)
1/3 cup chopped pecans

1/3 cup flaked coconut
1/2 pkg. 2-layer orange cake mix with
  pudding (about 2 cups)
1/3 cup butter or margarine
Vanilla ice cream

Preheat oven to 350°F (175°C). Spread undrained pineapple in bottom of an ungreased 10'' x 6'' baking dish. Spread apricot pie filling over pineapple. Sprinkle with pecans and coconut. Sprinkle dry cake mix evenly over pecans and coconut. Cut butter or margarine into small pieces and dot evenly over top of cake mix. Bake 55 to 60 minutes or until lightly browned. Serve warm in dessert bowls. Top with scoops of ice cream. Makes 6 to 8 servings.

How to Make Easy Ambrosia Cobbler

1/Layer crushed pineapple, apricot pie filling, chopped pecans and flaked coconut in baking dish. Sprinkle with orange cake mix and dot with butter or margarine.

2/After baking, spoon warm cobbler into bowls or stemmed dishes and top with generous scoops of vanilla ice cream or orange sherbet.

Mocha Macaroon Delights

With a dozen of these in the freezer, you'll never be caught short when guests drop in.

12 coconut macaroons
2 tablespoons creme de cacao or
  cold coffee

1 qt. coffee ice cream, softened
1/2 cup slivered almonds, toasted
Thick fudge ice cream topping

Crumble macaroons into a large bowl. Toss with creme de cocoa or coffee. Add ice cream and slivered almonds; mix well. Spoon into 12 paper baking cups in a muffin pan. Freeze firm. To serve, remove paper baking cups. Place frozen desserts in sherbet dishes. Top each serving with a swirl of fudge topping. Makes 12 servings.

Caramel Pecan Bars

Cut these oh-so-rich cookies into small bars.

1 (14-oz.) pkg. vanilla caramels
1/2 (14-oz.) can sweetened condensed milk
  (about 2/3 cup)
1 teaspoon vanilla extract

1 (15-oz.) roll refrigerated peanut butter
  cookie dough
1/2 cup pecan pieces

Preheat oven to 350°F (175°C). In a heavy medium saucepan, mix caramels and sweetened condensed milk. Stir over medium heat until caramels are melted and mixture is smooth. Remove from heat; stir in vanilla. Slice 2/3 of the cookie dough according to the package directions. Pat dough slices over bottom of a 9-inch square baking pan. Sprinkle with pecan pieces. Spread caramel mixture over cookie dough slices. Cut up remaining cookie dough. Dot over caramel mixture. Bake 30 minutes or until set. Makes twenty-seven 3'' x 1'' bars.

Lemon Cheesecake Squares

Delightful with your afternoon tea.

1 pkg. 2-layer lemon cake mix with pudding
1/2 cup butter or margarine, melted
1/2 cup finely chopped almonds, toasted
1 (8-oz.) pkg. cream cheese, softened
1/4 cup sugar

1 egg
2 tablespoons milk
1 tablespoon lemon juice
1 teaspoon vanilla extract

Preheat oven to 350°F (175°C). In a medium bowl, mix cake mix, melted butter or margarine and almonds. Reserve 1 cup cake mixture for topping. Pat remaining cake mixture into bottom of 9-inch square baking pan. Bake 15 minutes. In a small bowl, mix cream cheese, sugar, egg, milk, lemon juice and vanilla. Beat with electric mixer on high speed until just mixed and smooth. Spread over baked cake crust. Top with reserved cake mixture. Bake 30 minutes; cool. Cut into small squares. Refrigerate any leftovers. Makes about 50 squares.

Skillet Chocolate Sauce

Delicious served warm over ice cream or as a topping for brownies a la mode.

1/4 cup butter or margarine
1 cup sliced almonds
1 (6-oz.) pkg. chocolate chips (1 cup)

1/2 cup milk
1/4 cup creme de cacao or milk

In a medium skillet, melt butter or margarine. Add almonds. Stir over medium-high heat until nuts are toasted. Remove from heat. Stir in chocolate chips until partially melted. Add milk and creme de cacao. Stir over medium-low heat until mixture is smooth. Cool before serving. Makes 2 cups of sauce.

Rosy Fruit Compote

If you have time, chill the fruit mixture to blend the different flavors.

1 (10-oz.) pkg. frozen sweetened sliced
  strawberries, thawed
1 (10-oz.) pkg. frozen sweetened
  raspberries, thawed

1 (20-oz.) can cherry pie filling
1 tablespoon lemon juice
Dairy sour cream

Drain strawberries and raspberries; reserve 1/4 cup syrup from each fruit. In a large bowl, mix cherry pie filling, strawberries, raspberries, reserved syrups and lemon juice; stir gently. Refrigerate until serving time. Spoon into sherbet dishes. Top each serving with a dollop of sour cream. Makes 6 servings.

Holiday Honey-Rum Sauce

Add a little excitement to vanilla ice cream, gingerbread or warm canned plum pudding.

1/2 cup rum
1/2 cup mixed candied fruits and peels,
  finely chopped (about 4 oz.)

1/2 cup honey
1/4 cup chopped nuts

Pour rum over candied fruits and peels in a small bowl. Cover and let stand overnight or until ready to make sauce. In a saucepan, mix fruit-rum mixture and honey. Bring to a boil. Reduce heat and simmer uncovered 5 minutes. Stir in nuts. Serve warm. Makes 1-1/3 cups of sauce.

Rocky Road Pancakes

If your pancake mix already contains milk, egg and oil, see the variation below.

1/2 cup regular pancake mix
2 tablespoons unsweetened cocoa powder
1 tablespoon sugar
1/3 cup milk
1 egg
1 tablespoon vegetable oil

1/4 cup miniature marshmallows
1/4 cup pecan halves
Vegetable oil
Vanilla ice cream
Chocolate syrup
Chopped pecans, if desired

In a medium bowl, mix pancake mix, cocoa powder and sugar. Add milk, egg and oil. Whisk until fairly smooth; some lumps will remain. Stir in marshmallows and pecan halves. Brush a preheated griddle with oil. Using 1/4 cup batter for each pancake, cook on griddle until underside is browned and surface is bubbly. Turn and cook until other side is browned. Top with ice cream and chocolate syrup. Sprinkle with chopped pecans, if desired. Makes 4 pancakes.

Variation

To use a complete pancake mix that already contains milk, egg and shortening, omit the milk, egg and 1 tablespoon oil. Combine the pancake mix with cocoa powder, sugar and cinnamon. Add 1/2 cup water. Mix and bake as directed above.

Strawberry Yogurt Stack-Ups

These fabulous stacks are filled with creamy yogurt and juicy strawberries.

1 (10-oz.) pkg. frozen sweetened
   strawberries, thawed
1 cup regular pancake mix
Milk

Egg
Vegetable oil
1 (8-oz.) carton plain yogurt

Drain strawberries; reserve 1/4 cup syrup. Prepare pancake batter with milk, egg and oil according to package directions, substituting reserved strawberry syrup for 1/4 cup liquid called for on the package. Gently stir 1/4 cup drained strawberries into pancake batter; reserve remaining strawberries for filling and garnish. Brush a preheated griddle with oil. Using 1/4 cup of batter for each pancake, cook on griddle until underside is browned and surface is bubbly. Turn and cook until other side is browned. Using 2 pancakes for each stack, layer yogurt and strawberries between pancakes; reserve a few strawberries for garnish. Top each stack with a dollop of yogurt. Garnish with remaining strawberries. Makes 4 stack-ups.

Rocky Road Pancakes

Hawaiian Hotcakes

To make the batter with complete pancake mix, follow package directions and add 2 tablespoons sugar.

1 (8-oz.) can crushed pineapple
Sunshine Sauce, see below
1/2 cup shredded coconut
1 cup regular pancake mix
2 tablespoons sugar

Milk
Egg
Vegetable oil
Shredded coconut

Sunshine Sauce:
1/2 cup sugar
1 tablespoon cornstarch
Orange juice

Reserved pineapple juice
1 tablespoon lemon juice

Drain pineapple; reserve syrup for Sunshine Sauce. Prepare Sunshine Sauce; keep warm. Mix pineapple and 1/2 cup coconut in a small bowl; set side. Combine pancake mix and sugar in a medium bowl. Prepare pancake batter with milk, egg and oil according to package directions. Brush a preheated griddle with oil. Using 1/4 cup batter for each hotcake, pour onto hot griddle. Sprinkle each hotcake with about 2 tablespoons pineapple-coconut mixture. Cook until underside is browned and surface is bubbly. Turn and cook until other side is browned. Top hotcakes with Sunshine Sauce. Garnish with shredded coconut. Makes 8 hotcakes.

Sunshine Sauce:
Mix sugar and cornstarch in a small saucepan. Add orange juice to reserved pineapple syrup to make 1 cup. Stir into sugar mixture. Cook and stir over medium-high heat until sauce is thickened and bubbly. Remove from heat. Stir in lemon juice. Makes 1 cup of sauce.

Chocolate-Pecan Pancakes

Plan to serve dessert pancakes after a light supper.

1 cup regular pancake mix
Milk
Egg
Vegetable oil

1 teaspoon vanilla extract
1/2 (6-oz.) pkg. chocolate chips (1/2 cup)
1/4 cup chopped pecans
Creamy Topping, page 139, if desired

Prepare pancake batter with milk, egg and oil according to package directions. Stir in vanilla, chocolate chips and pecans. Brush a preheated griddle with oil. Using 1/4 cup batter for each pancake, cook on griddle until underside is browned and surface is bubbly. Turn and cook until other side is browned. Top with Creamy Topping, if desired. Makes 10 pancakes.

Variation

Cashew Scotchies: Substitute 1/2 cup butterscotch chips and 1/4 cup chopped cashews for the chocolate chips and pecans.

Sour Cream Cakes with Raisin Fluff Filling

Dried ground orange peel is available in the spice section of your supermarket.

Raisin Fluff Filling, see below
1 cup biscuit mix
2 tablespoons sugar
1/2 teaspoon ground nutmeg
1 egg

1/2 cup milk
1/2 cup dairy sour cream
Vegetable oil

Raisin Fluff Filling:
1 (4-oz.) carton frozen whipped topping, thawed
1/2 cup dairy sour cream
2 tablespoons orange juice

1/2 teaspoon ground nutmeg
1/2 teaspoon dried ground orange peel
1/4 cup raisins

Prepare Raisin Fluff Filling; set aside. In a medium bowl, mix biscuit mix, sugar, nutmeg, egg, milk and sour cream. Beat with a whisk until smooth. Brush a preheated griddle with oil. Using a scant 1/4 cup batter for each pancake, cook on griddle until underside is browned and surface is bubbly. Turn and cook until other side is browned. Spread 4 pancakes with Raisin Fluff Filling and cover with remaining pancakes. Top each stack with a dollop of filling. Makes 4 servings.

Raisin Fluff Filling:
In a medium bowl, mix whipped topping, sour cream, orange juice, nutmeg, and dried ground orange peel. Fold in raisins. Makes about 1-1/2 cups of filling.

Banana-Nut Pancakes

To make batter with complete pancake mix, follow package directions and add 1 tablespoon sugar.

Creamy Topping, see below
1 cup regular pancake mix
1 tablespoon sugar
Milk

Egg
Vegetable oil
1 medium banana, mashed
1/2 cup chopped pecans

Creamy Topping:
1 (3-oz.) pkg. cream cheese, softened
1/2 cup whipped topping

Prepare Creamy Topping; set aside. In a medium bowl, combine pancake mix and sugar. Prepare pancake batter with milk, egg and oil according to package directions. Stir in mashed banana and pecans. Brush a preheated griddle with oil. Using 1/4 cup batter for each pancake, cook on griddle until underside is browned and surface is bubbly. Turn and cook until other side is browned. Top with Creamy Topping. Makes 9 or 10 pancakes.

Creamy Topping:
In a small bowl, beat cream cheese with electric mixer on high speed until light and fluffy. Fold in whipped topping. Makes 1 cup of topping.

Impromptu Appetizers, Snacks & Beverages

Even though it doesn't take you long to prepare supper when you use ideas from this book, appetizers and a refreshing drink will keep everyone happy while you perform your magic.

Arrange an assortment of crackers on a small tray. In the middle of the tray place a container of semi-soft natural cheese spiced with garlic and herbs or pepper. One or two small bowls with garnishes such as chopped olives, caviar, chopped pickle, tiny cocktail shrimp or sardines will keep the gourmet snackers content until supper is ready. On a gala evening, fill a basket with fresh seasonal fruit, bread sticks, melba toast and several kinds of cheeses. A bottle of dry sherry and another of sweet sherry will provide the finishing touches.

Choose one of the following ideas for tonight's before-supper snack:
- Cut pita bread crosswise. Spread the bottom half with cheese spread from a jar. Add the pita top. Spread with softened butter and sprinkle with sesame seeds. Broil until the bread is browned and toasty. Cut into 2-inch pieces and arrange on a plate.
- Mix canned shoestring potatoes in a baking pan with melted butter, Parmesan cheese and fines herbes. Bake about 10 minutes or until warm. Serve in a wooden bowl.
- Make Boston sandwiches by spreading party rye bread with mayonnaise. Place a tomato slice and a thin onion slice on the mayonnaise. Top with another piece of party rye bread that's spread with mayonnaise.
- Fill a heatproof pitcher with hot spiced wine. Begin by simmering cinnamon sticks, whole nutmeg and whole allspice with apple juice. Then stir in white wine and heat through.
- Jazz up chicken or beef broth with dry sherry, a dash of Worcestershire sauce and a sprinkling of chives. Serve in soup cups as a first course.

Peppy Popcorn

Mound this popcorn in a basket and sprinkle it like croutons on cream soups.

3-1/2 qts. popped corn
1/4 cup butter or margarine, melted

1 envelope Italian salad dressing mix
2 tablespoons grated Parmesan cheese

Preheat oven to 300°F (150°C). Spread popcorn in a 13" x 9" baking pan. In a small saucepan, mix butter or margarine, Italian dressing mix and Parmesan cheese. Pour over popcorn; toss to mix well. Bake 10 minutes. Serve at once. Makes 3-1/2 quarts.

Variation:

Substitute one individual-serving-size envelope of dry onion soup mix for the Italian dressing and Parmesan cheese.

Maple Caramel Corn   *Photo on pages 142 and 143.*

About 6 tablespoons unpopped corn makes 3 quarts of popped corn.

3 qts. popped corn
1 (6-1/2-oz.) can salted cocktail peanuts
  (1-1/4 cups)
1/4 cup packed brown sugar
1/4 cup maple-flavored syrup

1/4 cup butter or margarine, melted
2 teaspoons vanilla extract
1/2 teaspoon salt
1 cup seedless raisins, plumped in
  hot water, drained

Preheat oven to 300°F (150°C). Toss together popcorn and peanuts in a 13" x 9" baking pan. In a small bowl, mix brown sugar, maple syrup, butter or margarine, vanilla and salt. Pour evenly over popcorn mixture. Toss to coat well. Bake 20 minutes, stirring occasionally. Add raisins; toss to mix well. Makes about 3-1/2 quarts.

Easy Nuts & Bolts

You'll enjoy TV more with a bowl of tasty-crunchy snacks.

3 tablespoons butter or margarine
1 tablespoon salad seasoning
1 teaspoon Worcestershire sauce
1/2 teaspoon garlic salt

1 cup pretzel sticks
1/2 cup peanuts
1/2 cup small shredded corn, wheat or
  rice cereal squares

Melt butter or margarine in a medium skillet. Stir in salad seasoning, Worcestershire sauce and garlic salt. Add pretzel sticks, peanuts and cereal squares. Cook and toss over medium-high heat until heated through and toasted. Makes about 2 cups.

Snacks and drinks for your next party are pictured on the following pages. Clockwise from top right: Maple Caramel Corn, above; Mulled Apple Punch, page 153; Three Cheese Balls, page 145; Shrimp Salad Rounds, page 145; Rio Bravo Taco Dip, page 144; Minted Lime Frosty, page 152; Margarita from Pitcher of Margaritas, page 154; Strawberry Slush, page 153.

Rio Bravo Taco Dip   *Photo on pages 142 and 143.*

Try taco chips, zucchini sticks, cherry tomatoes, sliced cauliflowerets and brussels sprouts for dippers.

1 (3-oz.) pkg. cream cheese, softened
1/2 cup mayonnaise or mayonnaise-style salad dressing
2 teaspoons lemon juice

2 hard-cooked eggs, coarsely chopped
3 tablespoons canned chopped green chilies
2 tablespoons taco seasoning mix
1/2 teaspoon garlic salt

In a small bowl, beat cream cheese, mayonnaise or salad dressing and lemon juice with electric mixer on medium speed until smooth. Stir in hard-cooked eggs, chilies, taco seasoning and garlic salt; mix well. Cover and refrigerate until serving time. Makes 1-1/2 cups of dip.

Hot Crab Dip

Use a chafing dish or a warming tray to keep the dip hot.

2 tablespoons butter or margarine
1 (3-oz.) pkg. cream cheese, cut in pieces
1/4 cup milk
1/4 cup shredded process American cheese

2 tablespoons chopped pimiento
Dash garlic salt
1/2 (6-oz.) pkg. frozen crabmeat, thawed, finely chopped

Melt butter or margarine in a small saucepan. Stir in cream cheese, milk, American cheese, pimiento and garlic salt. Cook and stir over low heat until cheeses are melted. Stir in crabmeat. Heat through. Makes about 3/4 cup of dip.

Ham-Artichoke Tidbits

Delectable little morsels to serve with your fancy cocktail picks.

1 (6-oz.) jar marinated artichoke hearts, drained
1 (4-oz.) pkg. whipped cream cheese with chives

5 or 6 thin slices rectangular baked or boiled ham

Cut large artichoke hearts in half; drain well on paper towels. Spread cream cheese generously on ham slices. Place 2 or 3 artichokes or artichoke halves at narrow end of each ham slice. Roll up jelly-roll fashion. Place ham rolls seam-side down on a platter. Cover and chill. To serve, carefully cut each ham roll with a serrated knife into 3/4-inch slices. Secure with cocktail picks. Place on a serving plate. Makes 20 to 24 appetizers.

Variation

Beef-Mushroom Tidbits: Use fresh or canned mushroom caps. Spread thin roast beef slices with semi-soft natural cheese spiced with garlic and herbs. Place mushroom caps at narrow end of each roast beef slice. Roll up, chill and cut as directed above.

Cheese-Chili Dip

Dip corn chips and vegetable dippers in this tasty rarebit sauce, or use it to top burgers and sandwiches.

1 (8-oz.) jar taco sauce
1 tablespoon all-purpose flour

2 cups shredded process American
  cheese (8-oz.)

Mix taco sauce and flour in a small saucepan. Stir until smooth. Cook and stir over medium-high heat until mixture thickens and bubbles. Add cheese. Stir until cheese is melted. Makes 1-1/2 cups of dip.

Three Cheese Balls   *Photo on pages 142 and 143.*

Complete your holiday appetizer platter with individual cheese balls.

1 (3-oz.) pkg. cream cheese, softened
1 cup shredded Cheddar cheese (4 oz.)
1/2 cup crumbled blue cheese

Chopped nuts
2 tablespoons butter or margarine

In a medium bowl, beat cream cheese, Cheddar cheese and blue cheese with electric mixer on high speed until blended. Chill. Shape into 1-inch balls. Roll each ball in chopped nuts. Melt butter or margarine in a large skillet. Add cheese balls. Cook over medium-high heat until toasted, about 3 minutes, turning often. Makes 15 appetizers.

Shrimp Salad Rounds   *Photo on pages 142 and 143.*

For a budget-stretcher, use tuna fish instead of shrimp.

1 (6-1/2-oz.) can shrimp, drained, cut up
1/2 cup shredded Monterey Jack cheese
1/4 cup chopped pimiento-stuffed
  green olives
1 teaspoon snipped chives
1/3 cup mayonnaise or mayonnaise-style
  salad dressing

1 tablespoon drained capers
1 teaspoon lemon juice
1 teaspoon Dijon-style mustard
1 (8-oz.) tube flaky-style refrigerated
  rolls (12 rolls)
Pimiento-stuffed green olives, sliced

Preheat oven to 400°F (205°C). In a medium bowl, mix shrimp, cheese, chopped olives, chives, mayonnaise or salad dressing, capers, lemon juice and mustard. Separate each roll into 3 layers. Place on an ungreased baking sheet. Top each piece with 1/2 tablespoon shrimp mixture. Bake 10 minutes or until golden brown. Garnish with olive slices. Serve hot. Makes 36 appetizers.

Frank Kabobs Deluxe

These tangy, glazed kabobs have a lot of style. Use your most elegant skewers.

1 (6-oz.) jar marinated artichoke
  hearts or crowns
1 (2-1/2-oz.) pkg. smoked sliced beef
1 (5-oz.) pkg. smoky cocktail link
  sausages

12 cherry tomatoes
4 dill pickle spears, cut in thirds

Preheat broiler. Drain artichokes; reserve marinade. Wrap artichokes in sliced beef. Thread alternately on 6 skewers: wrapped artichokes, cocktail links, cherry tomatoes and pickle pieces. Place on rack in broiler pan. Broil 5 inches from heat until heated through, about 5 minutes, turning and brushing frequently with reserved marinade. Makes 6 servings.

Swiss Ham Puffs

Enjoy them with cocktails or with a luncheon soup or salad.

1/2 cup mayonnaise or mayonnaise-style
  salad dressing
1 teaspoon prepared mustard
1 teaspoon prepared horseradish
1 (2-1/2-oz.) can deviled ham
1/4 cup drained pickle relish

2 hard-cooked eggs, chopped
1 tablespoon snipped fresh parsley
Dash onion salt
25 to 30 party rye bread slices
8 slices process American cheese

In a medium bowl, mix mayonnaise or salad dressing, mustard and horseradish. Stir in deviled ham, relish, eggs, parsley and onion salt. Preheat broiler. Place rye bread slices on baking sheets. Toast under broiler on both sides. Top each toasted rye slice with a scant tablespoon ham mixture. Cut each cheese slice into 4 squares. Top ham mixture with cheese squares. Broil 4 inches from heat 1 or 2 minutes or until cheese melts and puffs. Makes 25 to 30 appetizers.

South-of-the-Border Snack

Once you start nibbling on this version of nuts and bolts, you won't be able to stop.

1/2 cup butter or margarine
1 envelope taco seasoning mix
1 (8-oz.) jar soy nuts
2 cups pretzel sticks

2 cups small shredded corn cereal squares
1 (3-oz.) can chow mein noodles
2 cups corn chips

Preheat oven to 300°F (150°C). Melt butter or margarine in a saucepan. Stir in taco seasoning mix; set aside. In a large baking pan, mix soy nuts, pretzel sticks, cereal squares, noodles and corn chips. Pour taco seasoning mixture evenly over nut mixture. Toss gently to coat. Bake 20 minutes or until crisp and hot; cool. Store in airtight containers. Makes 10 to 12 cups.

Bob's Chicken Niblets

To use complete pancake mix, omit egg and 2 tablespoons oil; substitute water for the milk.

1/2 cup regular pancake mix
Dash ground ginger
1 egg, beaten
1/3 cup milk
2 tablespoons vegetable oil

1 uncooked chicken breast, boned,
   cut in 1-inch cubes
1/2 cup vegetable oil
Salt
Bottled sweet-sour sauce

In a medium bowl, stir together pancake mix, ginger, egg, milk and 2 tablespoons oil. Whisk until batter is fairly smooth; some lumps will remain. Dip chicken cubes in batter. Heat 1/2 cup oil in a large skillet. Cook chicken cubes in hot oil over medium-high heat until golden brown, 10 to 12 minutes, turning several times. Drain on paper towels. Sprinkle with salt. Serve on cocktail picks with sweet-sour sauce for dipping. Makes 4 servings.

How to Make Bob's Chicken Niblets

1/Use a sharp knife to cut boned chicken breast into 1-inch cubes.

2/Dip chicken cubes in batter. Fry in hot oil until golden brown.

Nutty Caramel Apples

Bourbon subtly flavors an old favorite!

1 tablespoon butter or margarine
3/4 cup caramel ice cream topping
1 tablespoon bourbon

2 apples, cored, cut in wedges
Chopped pecans

Melt butter or margarine in a small saucepan. Stir in ice cream topping and bourbon. Cook and stir over medium-low heat to blend and heat through. Remove from heat. Dip and roll apple wedges in caramel mixture and then in pecans. Serve in small dessert dishes. Makes 4 servings.

Sautéed Bananas

Popular in Latin America. A friend from El Salvador likes his with sweetened dairy sour cream.

2 tablespoons butter or margarine
1 firm banana, split lengthwise

2 tablespoons brown sugar

Melt butter or margarine in a medium skillet. Add banana halves. Sprinkle with brown sugar. Cook until bananas are heated through, turning occasionally. Cut in 1-inch pieces. Serve on wooden picks. Makes 2 servings.

Easy Chocolate Fudge

This no-fail method makes fudge set up every time.

2/3 cup sugar
1/4 cup evaporated milk
1 tablespoon butter or margarine
1/2 (6-oz.) pkg. chocolate chips
   (1/2 cup)

1/3 (4-oz.) bar German sweet chocolate
   (6 squares), chopped
1/2 cup chopped pecans
1/4 cup marshmallow creme

Butter a 9" x 5" loaf dish. In a small saucepan, combine sugar, evaporated milk and butter or margarine. Cook and stir until boiling. Stir in chocolate chips, German sweet chocolate, pecans and marshmallow creme. Continue to stir until smooth. Pour into buttered loaf dish; cool. Cut into squares. Makes about 2/3 pound.

Chocolate-Bourbon Balls

These keep well—if you hide them!

1 (6-oz.) pkg. chocolate chips (1 cup)
1/3 cup bourbon
3 tablespoons light corn syrup
2-1/2 cups vanilla wafer crumbs

1 cup chopped pecans
1/2 cup sifted powdered sugar
Granulated sugar

In a small saucepan, combine chocolate chips, bourbon and corn syrup. Cook and stir over low heat until chocolate chips are melted. In a large bowl, mix wafer crumbs, pecans and powdered sugar. Add chocolate mixture; mix well. Let stand about 30 minutes. Shape into 1-inch balls. Roll in granulated sugar. Let season several days in a tightly covered container. Makes about 36 balls.

Lemon Ice Balls

Very delicately flavored.

4 tablespoons butter or margarine
1/2 cup thawed frozen lemonade concentrate

1 (7-1/4-oz.) box vanilla wafers, crushed
About 1-1/2 cups powdered sugar

Melt butter or margarine in a small saucepan. Add lemonade concentrate. Cook and stir until heated through. In a large bowl, mix vanilla wafer crumbs and 1 cup powdered sugar. Add lemonade concentrate mixture to vanilla wafer mixture. Shape into 1-inch balls. Roll in remaining powdered sugar. Makes about 24 balls.

Peanut Butter & Fudge Sandwiches

Peanut butter and chocolate—how can you miss?

1 (6-oz.) pkg. peanut butter chips
   (1 cup)
1/2 cup light corn syrup
2 tablespoons butter or margarine,
   softened
4 cups crisp rice cereal

1 (6-oz.) pkg. chocolate chips (1 cup)
2 tablespoons butter or margarine,
   softened
1 tablespoon water
1/2 cup sifted powdered sugar

Butter an 8-inch square baking dish. In a large saucepan, combine peanut butter chips, corn syrup and 2 tablespoons butter or margarine. Cook and stir over medium heat until chips are melted and mixture is smooth. Add cereal. Stir to coat well with peanut butter mixture. Press half the cereal mixture into buttered baking dish. Chill. Set remaining cereal mixture aside. In a medium saucepan combine chocolate chips, 2 tablespoons butter or margarine and water. Cook and stir over medium heat until chips are melted. Remove from heat and stir in powdered sugar. Spread over chilled mixture. Spread remaining cereal mixture evenly over top. Press gently. Refrigerate about 1 hour or until firm. Cut into 1-1/2-inch squares. Makes about 24 squares.

Coconut-Mallow Squares

Make these for someone who has a hard-to-satisfy sweet tooth.

**1 (3-1/8-oz.) pkg. regular coconut cream
   pudding mix**
1/2 cup light corn syrup

1/2 (1-pt.) jar marshmallow creme
4 cups crisp rice cereal

Butter an 8-inch square baking dish. Combine pudding mix and corn syrup in a small saucepan. Stir over medium heat until mixture is blended and bubbly. Place marshmallow creme in a large bowl. Add hot syrup. Beat with a wooden spoon until blended. Fold in rice cereal. Turn into buttered baking dish. Cool before cutting into 2-inch squares. Makes about 16 squares.

How to Make Coconut-Mallow Squares

Beat hot pudding mixture into marshmallow creme, then fold in crisp rice cereal. Cool in buttered baking dish before cutting into bars.

Quick Cereal Snacks

- **Roll scoops of your favorite ice cream in crushed cereal.**
- **Dip bananas on sticks in chocolate or caramel sauce, then roll in crushed cereal.**
- **Coat cheese balls with crushed cereal.**
- **Dip bite-size shredded wheat or corn cereal in melted peanut butter chips.**
- **Layer canned pear halves with cream cheese and crushed cereal, then press two halves together.**
- **Spread apple slices with peanut butter, then sprinkle with crushed cereal.**

Minted Lime Frosty *Photo on pages 142 and 143.*

Sherbet, fruit and milk whipped to a froth is a refreshing after-dinner drink.

1 (12-oz.) jar minted pears
1/2 cup milk
2 tablespoons thawed frozen limeade
    concentrate

1 cup lime sherbet
Lemon slices
Green maraschino cherries

Drain pears; reserve 1/4 cup syrup. Combine drained pears, reserved syrup, milk and limeade in blender. Cover and process on high speed until mixture is smooth. Add sherbet. Cover and blend a few seconds at high speed just until thoroughly combined. Pour into glasses. Garnish with lemon twists and cherries. Serve at once. Makes 4 or 5 servings.

Sparkling Burgundy Coolers

Make this several weeks ahead and keep it in your freezer.

1 cup whipping cream (1/2 pint)
3/4 cup sugar
2-1/2 cups sparkling Burgundy wine

2 egg whites
1/2 teaspoon cream of tartar
1/4 cup sugar

In a medium saucpan, mix whipping cream and 3/4 cup sugar. Stir constantly over medium heat until sugar dissolves; cool. Stir in sparkling Burgundy. Pour mixture into a 13" x 9" baking dish. Cover and freeze 8 hours or overnight; mixture will not freeze firm. Place a large bowl in the freezer to chill. In a small bowl, beat egg whites with electric mixer on high speed until soft peaks form. Add cream of tartar, then gradually add 1/4 cup sugar, beating until stiff peaks form. Turn frozen Burgundy mixture into the large chilled bowl. Fold in beaten egg white mixture. Quickly return mixture to the baking dish. Cover and freeze. Before serving, stir to soften. Spoon mixture into brandy snifters and serve with straws. Makes 6 to 8 servings.

Raspberry Fizz

A delightfully different spur-of-the-moment drink.

1 scoop raspberry sherbet
1/2 cup red Dubonnet wine, chilled

Carbonated water, chilled

Scoop sherbet into a wine glass. Pour in wine. Fill glass with carbonated water. Serve with small straws. Makes 1 serving.

Strawberry Slush   *Photo on pages 142 and 143.*

Choose any frozen fruit packed in syrup and match it with flavored brandy or juice.

1/2 cup strawberry brandy or juice
4 cups crushed ice
1 (10-oz.) pkg. frozen sweetened
   strawberries packed in syrup

Fresh strawberries, if desired

Place brandy or juice, ice and frozen strawberries in blender. Cover and process on high speed until mixture is slushy. Spoon into sherbet glasses. Garnish with fresh strawberries, if desired. Serve immediately with spoons and short straws. Makes 6 servings.

Mulled Apple Punch   *Photo on pages 142 and 143.*

Spiced crab apples provide the tangy flavor and bright color.

2 (6-oz.) cans frozen apple juice
   concentrate, thawed
4 cups water

2 cups white grape juice
1 (14-oz.) jar spiced crab apples

In a large saucepan, mix apple juice concentrate, water and grape juice. Drain spiced crab apples; reserve 1/2 cup syrup. Add reserved syrup to apple juice mixture in saucepan. Bring to a boil; remove from heat. Place 1 crab apple in each of 12 punch cups or heat-resistant wine glasses. Fill with hot apple juice mixture. Makes 8 to 12 servings.

New Old-Fashioned

Every home bar should be equipped for mixing this alcohol-free refresher.

Orange wedge
Maraschino cherry
Pineapple chunk
1 sugar cube
3 dashes bitters

3 tablespoons strong tea
1 teaspoon lemon juice
Ice cubes
Carbonated water, chilled
Stick cinnamon

Spear orange wedge, cherry and pineapple chunk on a small skewer; set aside. Place sugar cube in an 8-ounce old-fashioned glass. Dash with bitters. Add tea and lemon juice; mix well. Add ice cubes and skewer with fruit. Fill glass with carbonated water; stir well. Serve with a cinnamon stick stirrer. Makes 1 serving.

Apricot Smoothie

As refreshing as it is pretty.

1 (8-oz.) can apricot halves, undrained
2 tablespoons thawed frozen orange juice
   concentrate

1/4 cup milk
Dash bitters
1 cup lemon sherbet

Place undrained apricots, orange juice concentrate, milk and bitters in blender. Cover and process on high speed until mixture is smooth. Add sherbet. Cover and blend a few seconds at high speed just until sherbet is combined with apricot mixture. Pour into glasses. Serve at once. Makes 2 or 3 servings.

Pink Princess Punch

Carbonated punch should be served immediately before it loses its sparkle.

Ice cubes
1 qt. white grape juice, chilled
1 (6-oz.) can frozen pink lemonade
   concentrate, thawed

1 lemonade can cold water
2 tablespoons grenadine syrup
2 (12-oz.) cans lemon-lime carbonated
   beverage, chilled

In a 2-1/2-quart pitcher, combine ice cubes, grape juice, lemonade concentrate, water and grenadine; mix well. Slowly pour in lemon-lime carbonated beverage. Stir and serve at once. Makes seventeen 1/2-cup servings.

Pitcher of Margaritas   *Photo on pages 142 and 143.*

An easy, no-fail method for the classic Mexican drink.

2 (6-oz.) cans frozen limeade
   concentrate, thawed
1-1/2 cups tequila
1/2 cup orange-flavored liqueur

2 (12-oz.) cans beer, chilled
Coarse salt
Crushed ice
Lime slices

Reserve 2 tablespoons limeade concentrate in a small saucer. Pour remaining limeade concentrate into a large pitcher. Add tequila and orange-flavored liqueur; stir well. Chill. Just before serving, slowly pour beer down side of pitcher. Dip rims of cocktail glasses into reserved limeade concentrate, then into salt, coating rims generously. Fill glasses 1/3 full of crushed ice. Fill with limeade mixture. Garnish with lime slices. Makes about 6 servings.

Spicy Cocoa Mocha Mix

Top hot Spicy Cocoa Mocha with whipped cream and a sprinkle of cinnamon.

4 cups nonfat dry milk powder
1 cup non-dairy coffee creamer
2-1/2 cups instant presweetened cocoa mix
1/2 cup instant coffee crystals

1-1/2 cups powdered sugar
1 tablespoon ground cinnamon
1 teaspoon ground allspice

In a large bowl, mix milk powder, coffee creamer, cocoa mix, coffee crystals, powdered sugar, cinnamon and allspice; mix well. To make 1 serving, measure 1/3 cup of dry mix into a mug. Fill mug with boiling water; stir. Store mix in a tightly covered container up to 2 months. Makes 6 cups dry mix or enough for 18 servings.

How to Make Spicy Cocoa Mocha Mix

1/Combine milk powder, coffee creamer, cocoa mix, instant coffee, powdered sugar and spices. Store in a large canister.

2/To make a cup of hot Spicy Cocoa Mocha, place 1/3 cup mix and a metal spoon in a mug. Pour boiling water over spoon to prevent mug from cracking.

Index

5.729053494413